MISSION:
WOLF RESCUE

Just like pet puppies, wolf pups love to chew, pull, and play with anything they can get their sharp little teeth on.

MISSION: WOLF RESCUE

ALL ABOUT WOLVES AND HOW TO SAVE THEM

BY KITSON JAZYNKA WITH NATIONAL GEOGRAPHIC EXPLORER DANIEL RAVEN-ELLISON

NATIONAL
GEOGRAPHIC
KiDS

WASHINGTON, D.C.

>>CONTENTS

6 Foreword

8 Introduction

10 Through a Wolf's Eyes

14 Chapter 1: The Wildest Howl

30 Chapter 2: Wolf Territory

46 Chapter 3: All in the Family

62 Chapter 4: On the Hunt

78 Chapter 5: Wolves and People

96 Chapter 6: Saving Wolves

112 Chapter 7: Take Action

118 Conclusion

120 Resources

124 Index

127 Credits

A wolf pack is a family unit, with many similarities to human families.

MISSION: ANIMAL RESCUE

SAVE ANIMALS · SAVE THE WORLD

Lions and *Tigers* and *Polar Bears*—oh, my! Be sure to check out the other titles in the Mission: Animal Rescue series. Coming soon to bookshelves near you.

MISSION: ANIMAL RESCUE

At National Geographic we know how much you care about animals. They enrich our planet—and our lives. Habitat loss, hunting, and other human activities are threatening many animals across the globe. The loss of these animals is a loss to humanity. They have a right to our shared planet and deserve to be protected.

With your help, we can help save animals—through education, through habitat protection, and through a network of helping hands. I firmly believe the animals of the world will be safer with us on their side.

Throughout this book and the other books in the Mission: Animal Rescue series, you'll see animal rescue activities just for kids. If you go online at kids.nationalgeographic.com/mission-animal-rescue, you can join a community of kids who wants to help animals as much as you do. Look for animal rescue videos, chats with explorers, and more. Plus, don't miss the dramatic stories of animal rescues in *National Geographic Kids* magazine.

We share our Earth with animals. Helping them means helping our planet and protecting our future.

Together we can do it.

—Daniel Raven-Ellison, *Guerrilla Geographer and National Geographic Explorer*

YOUR PURCHASE SUPPORTS ANIMALS AND THEIR HABITATS

The National Geographic Society is a nonprofit organization whose net proceeds support vital exploration, conservation, research, and education programs. Proceeds from this book will go toward the Society's efforts to support animals and their habitats. From building bomas for big cats to protect their wild territory to studying elephants and how they communicate to exploring wild places to better understand animal habitats, National Geographic's programs help save animals and our world. Thank you for your passion and dedication to this cause. To make an additional contribution in support of Mission: Animal Rescue, ask your parents to consider texting ANIMAL to 50555 to give ten dollars. See page 128 for more information.

A captive gray wolf enjoys a spring day in Montana, U.S.A.

>> INTRODUCTION

HELP SAVE THE WOLF

Whether you've heard it in a movie or during a visit to Yellowstone National Park, we all know the unforgettable howl of the wolf. But do you know what those howls mean? Humans think of the howl as a powerful symbol, an electrifying noise that makes others stop and wonder. But wolves howl as a way to communicate with other wolves. They howl by themselves, back and forth across a valley, or in a group, to say something as simple as "Where are you?" or as fearsome as "Stay away!"

Wolves and humans have a complicated, shared history. Wolves have been a part of human culture for as far back as we can study. We have even bred wolves with dogs and brought them into our homes as pets. But today, some wolves—like red wolves and Mexican gray wolves—are in trouble.

Though wolves are idolized around the world as a symbol of the wilderness, controversy surrounding management of wild wolves and turf wars over habitat are going on around the world. And even though, for some reading this book, that may be happening in areas far from where you live, it is still an important issue that affects the entire planet. Can you imagine a world without wolves?

Together we can help save the wolf. All around us, many different kinds of people are working to learn about the complicated and elusive life of these endangered canines and their habitats. The more of us that share the message of the wolf—by howling with our own voices, or by simply learning and sharing information—the more success we'll have protecting this fascinating and beautiful animal.

At the end of each chapter in this book, you'll find rescue activities. By doing these activities, you'll learn more about wolves and help share the message about the importance of these creatures. Each activity will help you learn how to help save wolves. But don't be modest!

Let out a long howl and read on to learn how to make your voice loud. Let's save wolves!

>>THROUGH A WOLF'S EYES

THE BLACK WOLF

A **brutal winter wind sweeps snow across the Lamar Valley in Yellowstone National Park. The ragged *caw* of a raven cuts through the frigid gusts. Trotting through the tall grass that spikes the snow, the black wolf is on a mission. His lonely howls have been answered by a potential mate. Finding her consumes him.**

He spots the pretty young charcoal-colored female he's come to court. He can't take his yellow eyes off her as she lopes through the snow to greet him. But danger lurks. Her father is the powerful leader of one of the biggest wolf packs in Yellowstone National Park—the Druids. The black wolf is an outsider. Strolling into Druid territory is asking to be attacked. He tries to blend in, not wanting to be noticed. But she's enthusiastic—giddy even—leaping and bounding with delight to meet him.

It's too late to retreat unnoticed. He's already been spotted. The young female's father, a huge graying wolf, is on his way. Impressive and powerful, the pack leader is known as #21. When the black wolf sees the attacker running at him, flanked by another large Druid male, he must make a choice: run or risk death by standing and facing the challenge. A rebel at heart, he comes up with an original plan.

NATIONAL GEOGRAPHIC

THE RISE OF BLACK WOLF

MOVIE STAR

Filmmaker Bob Landis followed Black Wolf, also known as #302, for years. The result was a National Geographic documentary called *The Rise of Black Wolf* that showed the world how one rebellious canine survived in our wild, modern world.

Yellowstone wolf #302 (left) lived a longer than average life by avoiding conflict.

He runs toward #21, tucks his tail, lowers his eyes, and crouches in surrender.

But his attempt at submission fails. The leader of the Druids slams the young wolf down with deadly force and leaps on him, biting with sharp fangs at the black wolf's stomach and throat. The young wolf doesn't stand a chance.

But #21 seems to have a policy against killing male invaders. After ten minutes, he lets his victim slip out from under him. Bitten, scratched, and bleeding, the black wolf runs straight for the road.

Most wolves won't go near the black ribbon road that curls through the park. They know it's dangerous. His sides heaving and his face covered with snow, the black wolf turns and looks back. The Druid leader stops chasing when he sees the road, an unlikely safety zone for the black wolf.

Challengers like the black wolf usually fight for dominance or move on. But not this wolf. Alone again, he stops along the side of the road, looking back toward the Druid's rich, wide valley. He howls out a plea to the charcoal female. She responds with a hopeful howl.

He lives out the winter and most of the next year near the road. She spends more time with him and less with her father's pack. The black wolf retreats to the road whenever #21 is around.

Most wolves in this situation would become a "pair bond" and start their own pack. But the black wolf doesn't seem to want to lead his own pack. He passes the time without commitment, free of responsibility, avoiding conflict as much as he can.

HAIR-RAISING ENCOUNTER

Early one morning, the *whoosh* of a small helicopter interrupts the black wolf's travels at the outskirts of the Druid territory. He's still an outsider, but at least he's become a regular outsider. The aspen trees blow wildly and snow sprays into the air as the helicopter swoops low and chases the wolf down. The yellow beast is loud and terrifying.

As he tries to escape, a dart pierces his skin through his thick winter coat. He collapses as the helicopter lands in a clearing nearby. Wolf biologist Doug Smith jumps out of the helicopter and runs toward the wolf.

The snow settles. Tranquilized, the wolf doesn't feel the biologist's kind hands taking his measurements,

checking his teeth, tagging him, and strapping a radio-transmitting collar around his neck. When he wakes up, the biologist and the yellow beast have vanished.

Now he's collared and has an identification number: Yellowstone wolf #302. Humans will study his movement and behavior. The ordeal doesn't keep him down for long. He shakes it off and trots over a hill toward the broad valley. Over the next few years, the black wolf teaches wolf biologists in Yellowstone that these amazing canines don't always play by the rules.

PACK LEADER

Eventually the black wolf becomes a father. Whenever #21 is out on the hunt, the black wolf sneaks into the Druid den to visit his pups. He also travels west to visit

A wolf might howl to start a hunt, to celebrate a feast, or to connect with a member of his pack.

his natal Leopold Pack to help his parents with their new pups, his youngest siblings. It's 50 miles (80 km) round-trip to the Leopolds' Blacktail Plateau from the Druids' Lamar Valley and back again.

Another year goes by and #21 and his female partner die. The loss leaves the Druids desperate for a leader. Another wolf appears and takes over. The black wolf joins the Druids as a subordinate. But the pack is forced to retreat to another territory after harassment from a larger, neighboring pack. The Druids later reclaim their territory, but #302 leaves the pack in early 2009, setting out with five young wolves.

In his last year of life, #302 and the five youngsters join up with three females to form the Blacktail Plateau Pack. Now he's the leader of a pack for the first time in his life. The black wolf claims a territory for his pack on the Blacktail Plateau, a free stretch of land with abundant prey. He witnesses the birth of his first litter as a pack leader.

Most wolves in the wild don't live past five years old. The black wolf is almost ten and has survived attacks, exile, and famine. He's grown into a heavily muscled hunter and has brought down hundreds of elk. It's likely the black wolf survived so long because he avoided conflict with other male wolves. After years of breaking the rules, he leads a pack like a pro. The new pack has a bright future.

ABOUT 18 WOLF PACKS LIVE IN YELLOWSTONE NATIONAL PARK, OR SPEND TIME THERE.

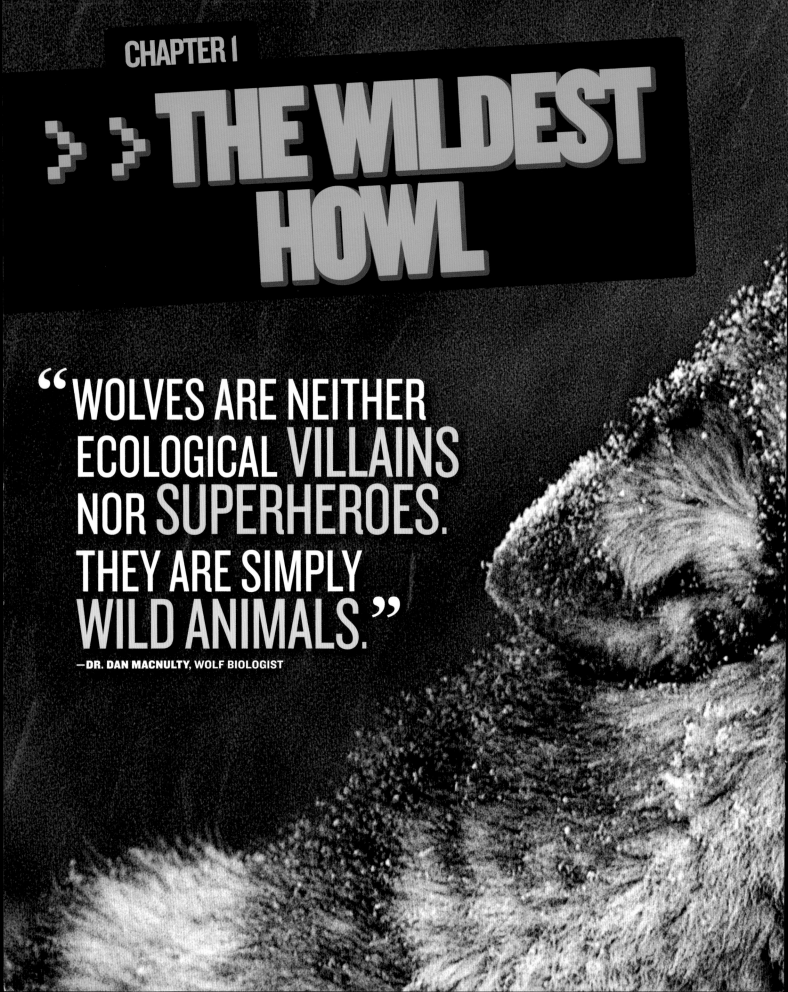

CHAPTER 1

>> THE WILDEST HOWL

" WOLVES ARE NEITHER ECOLOGICAL VILLAINS NOR SUPERHEROES. THEY ARE SIMPLY WILD ANIMALS. "

—DR. DAN MACNULTY, WOLF BIOLOGIST

It's a myth that wolves howl at the moon, but they tend to howl more when it's lighter at night, which usually happens when there's a full moon.

A young wolf crouches behind a snow-covered log under towering aspen trees. He waits. Then with a powerful leap, he launches a furry, 100-pound (45 kg) ambush, spraying snow in every direction.

He wraps massive clawed forepaws around his startled brother, who growls and grabs a mouthful of thick, coarse fur in a mock counterattack. They roll, romp, snarl, and chase. Then the wild animals flop, thump their tails on the ground, and look at each other with eyes that seem to laugh. Every panting breath shoots a puff of vapor in the frigid air.

WILD WOLVES

Packs of fierce, smart, and adaptable wolves like these have survived in the wild on nearly every continent of our planet for hundreds of thousands of years, raising their pups, hunting their prey, playing, and filling night skies with their magnificent voices. Have you ever heard a wild wolf howl? It's one of wildlife's most electrifying sounds. *Arrooooo!*

Stealth hunters built for survival, a wolf's round-tipped, upright ears might remind you of a German shepherd dog but with the fur of an Alaskan malamute. A wolf is taller than either of those domestic dogs. He's got a leaner body type, a wider head, massive jaws for crushing bones, a bigger muzzle, and a coat designed to keep him warm in some of the Earth's most frigid climates. His legs are long, thin, and close together, giving him a lanky look.

HUNTING HARDWARE

A wolf's jaws hold 42 large teeth (that's 10 more than adult humans have), including sharp, inch-long (2.5 cm) canines to rip or puncture his prey's thick skin.

WOLVES ARE THE LARGEST WILD CANINES IN THE WORLD, WEIGHING BETWEEN 65 AND 140 POUNDS (30 TO 65 KG).

A male wolf shows his playful side in the tall grass.

Arctic Ocean

Greenland
(DENMARK)

Alaska
(U.S.)

CANADA

NORTH AMERICA

UNITED
STATES

NORWAY
SWEDEN
FINLAND
ESTONIA
LATVIA
LITHUANIA
GERMANY
POLAND
BELARUS
FRANCE
UKRAINE
EUROPE
ITALY
ROMANIA
GEORGIA
PORTUGAL
SPAIN
BULGARIA
ARMENIA
AZERBAIJAN
GREECE
TURKEY
LEBANON
SYRIA
ISRAEL
IRAN
JORDAN
KUWAIT
BAHRAIN
LIBYA
EGYPT
SAUDI
ARABIA
OMAN
YEMEN

RUSSIA

KAZAKHSTAN

ASIA

MONGOLIA

NORTH
KOREA

UZBEKISTAN
KYRGYZSTAN
TURKMENISTAN
TAJIKISTAN

PAKISTAN

CHINA

BHUTAN
NEPAL

INDIA

Pacific
Ocean

Atlantic
Ocean

Pacific
Ocean

AFRICA

ETHIOPIA

EQUATOR

SOUTH
AMERICA

Indian
Ocean

AUSTRALIA

Countries that share the wolves'
present-day range are labeled.
Countries too small to be labeled
are numbered:

1 Czech Republic
2 Slovakia
3 Hungary
4 Slovenia
5 Croatia
6 Bosnia & Herzegovina
7 Serbia
8 Montenegro
9 Kosovo
10 Macedonia
11 Albania

Approximate present-day wolf range

Former additional range

ANTARCTICA

Range includes all subspecies of **Canis lupus,** except those
of the domesticated dog:

Alaskan tundra wolf, Alexander Archipelago wolf, Arabian wolf, arctic wolf, Baffin
Island wolf, eastern timber wolf, Egyptian wolf, Eurasian wolf, Great Plains wolf
(buffalo wolf), Greenland wolf, Hudson Bay wolf, Iberian wolf, Indian wolf, Italian
wolf, Labrador wolf, Mackenzie Valley wolf, Mexican wolf, northern Rocky
Mountains wolf, red wolf, steppe wolf, Tibetan wolf, tundra wolf, Vancouver Island
wolf, and Yukon wolf

| 0 | | 2,000 | miles |
| 0 | | 2,000 | kilometers |

His molars can crush a moose's femur (upper hind leg bone) in fewer than eight chomps. From the tip of his tail to his nose, a male wolf can be nearly 7 feet (2 m)—that's almost as long as basketball player Shaquille O'Neal stands tall. A wolf has gigantic feet with flexible toes (four on each foot) for agility and speed over uneven terrain. He walks, trots, lopes, or runs on long legs depending on how fast he needs to get where he's going.

FEROCIOUS FEATURES

Wolves, like other predators including bears, cats, bats, and seals, are part of the order of animals referred to as Carnivora. The wolf is the largest member of the Canidae—or dog—family, of which 39 species still exist, including the fox, coyote, jackal, wild dog, and domestic dog. Scientists currently recognize three species of wolves: the gray wolf, the red wolf, and the eastern wolf. Subspecies of the gray wolf are found all over the world and include the rare Mexican gray wolf and the arctic

WOLVES USE THEIR VOICES, THEIR PAWS, EYE CONTACT, AND EVEN BODY ODOR TO SAY, "BETTER LUCK NEXT TIME," "KEEP OUT," OR "DON'T EVEN THINK ABOUT EATING THAT."

gray. Once common throughout the southeastern United States, populations of smaller red wolves can now be found wild only in protected areas of North Carolina.

Covered in thick, rough hair, a wolf can range in color from yellowish to reddish, gray, black, and even pure white in arctic populations. And just as the gray wolf is not always gray, the red wolf can be tan or brown, often with reddish highlights around its ears and black along its back. Even though sharp-eyed wolves most closely resemble domestic dogs like German shepherds and Alaskan malamutes, a fluffy bichon frise or a roly-poly French bulldog is just as closely related to the wolf. Some scientists believe that domesticated dogs evolved *from* the gray wolf. Others believe that wolves and dogs share only a common ancestor that they each evolved from separately.

FAMILY LIFE

Wolves have a lot in common with our pets at home, like their desire to live within a pack. Your family is

(continued on p. 22)

ANIMAL SUPERPOWERS — WOLF POWER

SOME PEOPLE THINK WOLVES ARE ECOLOGICAL ANGELS THAT CAN SAVE AN ENTIRE ECOSYSTEM—RIGHT DOWN TO BEETLES, FISH, AND GRASS.

SOME PEOPLE THINK ALL WOLVES ARE ECOLOGICAL GANGSTERS THAT DO NOTHING BUT KILL.

BUT IN FACT, LIKE OTHER WILD ANIMALS, WOLVES ARE *NEITHER* SUPERHEROES *NOR* VILLAINS.

SUPERSTAR OF YELLOWSTONE

Travel the highway that cuts through Yellowstone National Park's lush Lamar Valley and you never know what you might see—bison, grizzly bears, otters, pronghorn, and (you guessed it!) wolves. Since the reintroduction of wolves into the Wyoming, U.S.A., park in the mid-1990s, tourists from all over the world have staked out the sides of this road, hoping to catch a glimpse of one of the valley's most famous residents—the leader of the Lamar Canyon wolf pack—the beautiful, tawny-eared wolf #823, also known as the "'06 Female," because of the year she was born. You could say she was a supermodel. During her life, she was one of the most photographed animals in the park's history.

Known as a fierce mother (once holding off grizzly bears from snatching her pups) and hunter (she was known to take elk down by herself)—'06 led her highly visible pack for years in the park's northern Rocky Mountains. She also contributed to science, wearing a $4,000 GPS (global positioning system) tracker on a collar. The tracking device sent scientists details about her location via satellite several times a day.

But wolves don't know state or park boundaries. And they don't know about the politics of wildlife management. In the fall of 2012, '06 couldn't have known that, for the first time in decades, it was legal to hunt wolves in Wyoming. That December, she ventured 15 miles (24 km) outside of the park into Wyoming. A hunter shot and killed her. Her death started a nationwide debate among scientists and state wildlife management about protection for wolves.

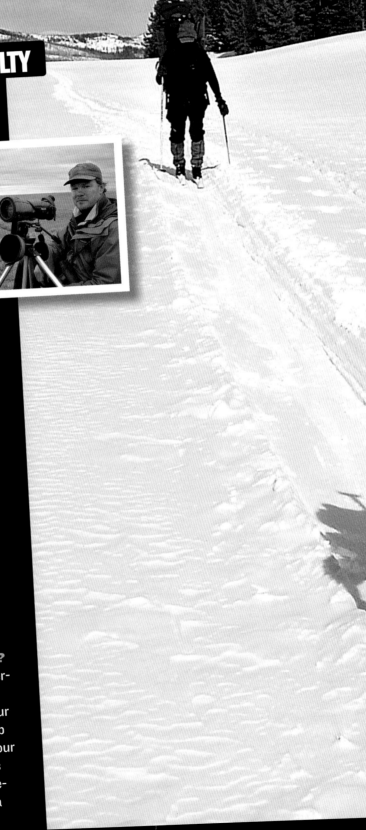

>> EXPLORER INTERVIEW

DR. DAN MACNULTY

BORN: ARLINGTON HEIGHTS, ILLINOIS, U.S.A.
JOB TITLE: ASSISTANT PROFESSOR OF WILDLIFE ECOLOGY, UTAH STATE UNIVERSITY, DEPARTMENT OF WILDLAND RESOURCES
JOB LOCATIONS: LOGAN, UTAH, U.S.A., AND YELLOWSTONE NATIONAL PARK
YEARS WORKING WITH WOLVES: 18
MONTHS A YEAR IN THE FIELD: 1

How are you helping to save wolves?
By providing factual information on wolf biology and wolf-prey interactions to the general public and decision makers. Most people assume that the predatory power of wolves is unlimited. I work to dispel that myth with facts gathered from my long-term research of Yellowstone wolves.

Favorite thing about your job?
I relish the freedom to pursue research that I think is important. I also enjoy using the results of that research to educate the public about wildlife and wildlands. I especially enjoy providing information that challenges entrenched assumptions.

Best thing about working in the field?
Being able to witness the drama of nature and the lives of nonhuman animals.

Worst thing about working in the field?
Being outsmarted by wolves.

How can kids prepare to do your job one day?
Get into wild nature and explore! Develop your observational skills by learning how to identify the plants and animals you find. Keep a journal and record your observations. Writing is an important part of the job because it's the main way we inform others about our work. Learning how to write well is as important as learning field skills. Volunteer for a wolf- or wildlife-related research project and learn firsthand from a professional wildlife biologist.

One of my favorite memories involves watching the formation of Yellowstone's first wild wolf pack after the wolf reintroduction.

What is the easiest way to walk through snow in Yellowstone? On skis! Dr. MacNulty heads out to watch wolves hunt bison in the park.

your dog's pack. Your pooch might not get a place at the dinner table, but you make sure he gets food, water, shelter, and care every day. Members of a wolf pack do the same for each other.

A wolf's ability to survive depends on his ability to get along with his pack, which is made up of parents (the breeding male and female) and their offspring. Survival also has to do with biological success. How long can the wolf survive—stay fed and not get killed during a hunt—to bring more offspring into the world year after year?

Speaking of eating, have you ever heard the saying "hungry like a wolf"? Hunger is a big part of a wolf's existence. He might go for weeks without eating. Unlike a human's digestive system, a wolf's body can handle long periods with very little food. He can exist for months eating only bones. On the other hand, when the stealth hunter is successful, his stomach

>> EXPERT TIPS

Check out wolf expert Dr. Dan MacNulty's tips for studying wolves at home or in your backyard:

1 Learn as much as you can about wolves, including the evidence of their presence in the wild, like tracks, scat (poop), remains of kills, howling, etc. Be able to distinguish appearance, signs, and vocalizations of wolves from those of other carnivores.

2 Get involved in a wildlife project.

3 When observing wolves, do not approach them. Not only is this dangerous, but they'll detect you and flee. Make sure to be patient and quiet.

>> ANIMAL RESCUE!

WOLF WRITER

Growing up, wolf biologist and nature lover Dan Stahler sat behind his desk in the seventh grade, in Lyndon, Vermont, U.S.A., annoyed at having to write another lab report. What he didn't know yet was that he was preparing himself for a career in the wilderness helping to save wolves.

As a wolf biologist in Yellowstone National Park for the past 18 years, Stahler studies wolf behavior and the species' impact on the environment. He counts wolf pups, watches how the pack takes care of their young, and observes wolves interacting with grizzly bears and bison. He makes observations and records data while traveling on airplanes, on skis, on horseback, or on his own two feet.

Stahler shares what he learns by writing about wolves. He writes about scientific topics ranging from wolf and scavenger interactions (like between wolves, ravens, coyotes, and grizzly bears) to the importance of family relationships and behaviors that are important to the success of wolf packs. Most of Stahler's writing appears in scientific journals, but he also writes reports every year on the ecology and behavior of Yellowstone's wolves.

By sharing these animal stories, Stahler hopes to help others better understand these charismatic, yet controversial, creatures and their importance in nature.

Like humans, dogs, and many other animals, wolves use body language to express how they feel. A tail straight up in the air means "I'm in charge here."

Wolves in Denali National Park in Alaska, U.S.A., feast on a moose after a kill. Wolf kills provide important leftovers for scavengers including grizzly bears.

can hold more than 20 pounds (9 kg) of meat—as much as a Thanksgiving turkey.

When it comes to the average wolf's diet, it's all about meat, but we're not talking hot dogs and hamburgers. Wolves eat large, even-toed hoofed mammals, like deer, elk, moose, or bison, also referred to as ungulates. Wolves supplement their ungulate diet with smaller prey like mice and other rodents, rabbits, raccoon, beaver, and leftovers from other predators' kills.

The meat wolves eat gives them almost all the water they need. A wolf might lap water from a stream or snarf snow to cool himself down after an unsuccessful hunt (otherwise he'd be hydrating by eating). A female wolf will drink free-flowing water if she has pups to nurse. This is why, some scientists believe, wolf dens are usually found close to running water.

KEYSTONE SPECIES

You might not think that the presence of a wolf could impact the life of a bird, a fish, or the aspen trees that shade his den. But wolves may have a big impact on their ecosystems (the communities of living and non-living things where any of us live). One big difference between domesticated dogs and wolves is that some scientists consider wolves to be a keystone species. A keystone is the part of a group on which everything else depends. Take away that one thing and the ecosystem changes.

Some scientists believe this happened in Yellowstone National Park when wolves disappeared in 1929 after decades of extermination by human hunters and habitat loss. Because elk were no longer afraid of being eaten by wolves, they got lazy. They hung around the streams

WOLVES VS. DOMESTIC DOGS

	WOLVES		DOMESTIC DOGS
SIZE	Up to 7 feet (2 m), and up to 140 pounds (65 kg)		Can vary by the breed
PHYSICAL TRAITS	Longer snout, stronger jaws, larger teeth		Rounder head, shorter legs
PREY	Meat and ungulates like elk, moose, deer, and more—even the hooves!		Dog treats and dog chow, but not chocolate, grapes, onions, or bones
BEHAVIOR	Like to be around other wolves		Like to be around people

ONE SIGN OF A WOLF DEN IS THE PUPS' CHEW TOYS—LIKE BONES AND STICKS—SCATTERED ALL OVER THE PLACE AND COVERED IN TINY BITE MARKS.

and gobbled tender willow tree buds, preventing trees from growing, season after season.

Now there were fewer spots for songbirds to nest. Without shady trees, the stream water got too warm for the fish. So many hooves in the muddy stream banks caused the stream to widen. Beavers had fewer places to build their dams and lodges. Without competition from wolves, coyotes took over, feasting on small mammals, taking food away from golden eagles, bald eagles, badgers, and foxes.

When reintroduced to the park in 1995, wolves helped strengthen the ecosystem. Wolves helped sustain other animals that live on carrion (carcasses of animals left after a kill), like grizzly bears, eagles, and coyotes. As carrion breaks down and disintegrates into the earth, the leftovers help distribute valuable nutrients and minerals back into the soil.

This is what some scientists believe. Nobody really knows if the presence of a wolf can improve the life of a fish or a beaver, but a lot of people believe it does.

Until the 1970s, wolves were on a path to being entirely wiped out in the United States, Europe, and Asia. In North America, pioneers in the 1800s killed wolves, influenced by old myths they brought from Europe that cast the wild animals as malicious killers. They exterminated wolves as they cleared the land for agriculture. Wolves have been poisoned, trapped, and shot throughout American history, all while their relatives—our beloved family dogs—were pampered in our homes.

Wolves depend heavily on their senses, like smelling, seeing, and hearing, to stay aware of what's going on around them.

But wolves around the world today are experiencing a comeback. Once eradicated, in the past 20 years wolves have become a symbol of the underdog endangered species. Stories of conservation successes are featured in magazines and newspapers with stunning photographs of beautiful, elusive wolves. Thrilling wildlife documentaries share the secrets of wolves' lives. Hundreds of nonprofit organizations have been formed around the world to protect wolves and educate the public about their importance.

There are still many differing opinions about how to handle wolves—from the differing points of view of scientists, ranchers, animal activists, hunters, and environmental conservationists. And in some areas, like Mexico and Japan, there has been very little recovery. But overall, scales have tipped in favor of the beloved wolf.

>> ANIMAL RESCUE!

WHO'S FOR DINNER? <<<

A wolf in Yellowstone National Park chows down on an elk carcass.

Every time a GPS-collared elk dies in Yellowstone National Park, scientists get an email. Biologists in the field then race to the scene of the "crime" and try to figure out whodunit. They try to piece together clues about what or who killed the elk—before it's consumed. Technology alerts them to the kill, but at the scene of the crime, they have to rely on their own senses to figure out the cause of death. Puncture wounds on the neck suggest a wolf kill. A carcass hidden in the underbrush points to a cougar.

It's all part of a study to determine the impact of wolves on their prey population. A lot of people think wolves are powerful ecological agents that have the power to kill off an entire population of prey. But could wolves really do that? Tracking radio-collared wolves and elk in Yellowstone, a team of North American scientists have set out to answer that complicated question.

While wolves have played a role in the decline of elk numbers, there are many other factors. Drought and human hunters killing healthy breeding-age female elk have taken a heavy toll on the declining elk population. Grizzly bears and cougars are major predators of elk calves, and cougars also kill adult female elk.

Like many things related to wolves, it's a complicated story. Scientists are helping to figure it out, replacing speculation about the impact of wolves on Yellowstone elk with facts. But for now, the question of how large a role wolves play in the story of the Yellowstone elk is still unanswered.

> > RESCUE ACTIVITIES

LIVING LIKE A WOLF

Have you heard the phrase "a wolf in sheep's clothing"? This is an old cautionary saying that means you cannot always trust the way someone or something looks. It also implies that wolves are bad and not to be trusted. When you do this challenge you'll turn this old saying on its head, giving you the opportunity to tell people all about wolves.

NOVICE

WATCH WOLVES TO SEE HOW THEY BEHAVE. Study their body language. A good place to start is by observing your family or neighborhood dog. Since dogs and wolves are related, they make a lot of the same movements.

RESEARCH WOLF BODY LANGUAGE by heading to the local zoo, watching videos online, checking out books, or more! Look carefully at their body language and start mirroring this in your own movements.

HOWL LIKE A WOLF! A wolf's howl can be heard as far as 10 miles (16 km) away. How far can you make your howl heard? Telephones and the Internet are allowed!

EXTREME

BUILD YOURSELF AN OUTDOOR DEN THAT YOU CAN USE AS YOUR BASE. Remember, wolves make actual dens only when they have pups to look after. When they do, wolves pick a place close to water and make space for pups to grow and play.

INSTEAD OF BURROWING INTO THE GROUND OR FINDING A CAVE (both of these can be highly dangerous), gather together branches, cardboard boxes, and sheets to make your hideout. Can you make it big enough for you and your friends?

WOLVES NORMALLY LIKE HIDDEN SPOTS in the forest, but your den could welcome family and friends with a sign, fun decorations, and more!

BE A HUMAN IN WOLF'S CLOTHING BY CREATING A WOLF COSTUME. Make yourself a wolf tail out of fuzzy material. Clip it onto the back of your pants and casually start wearing it around, as if having a tail is perfectly normal.

USE SOME HEAVY PAPER TO MAKE A WOLF MASK. Think carefully about how to make your mask. Your wolf could look friendly or scary, it all depends on how you draw your mouth and eyes. Use fake fur to make your mask feel real.

DARE TO USE YOUR BEST SEWING SKILLS? Make yourself an entire wolf costume, including a fake fur jacket, pants, gloves, and shoe-cover paws. You can use your outfit to explore your territory and hunt for food.

To howl your message, you may need to do something strange to surprise your audience.

1 Grab their attention! Plan to show off your project in an unexpected and unusual place. Or make your project super-size or ridiculously tiny.

2 The more the merrier. Getting a pack of friends to help you gets the project done faster and can be more fun!

3 When anyone stops to ask you why you are behaving like a wolf, be sure to explain what you are doing and why. By showing people what wolves are like, you're helping to spread the message!

CHAPTER 2

>> WOLF TERRITORY

Aroooo! A wolf's howl can be heard up to ten miles (16 km) away.

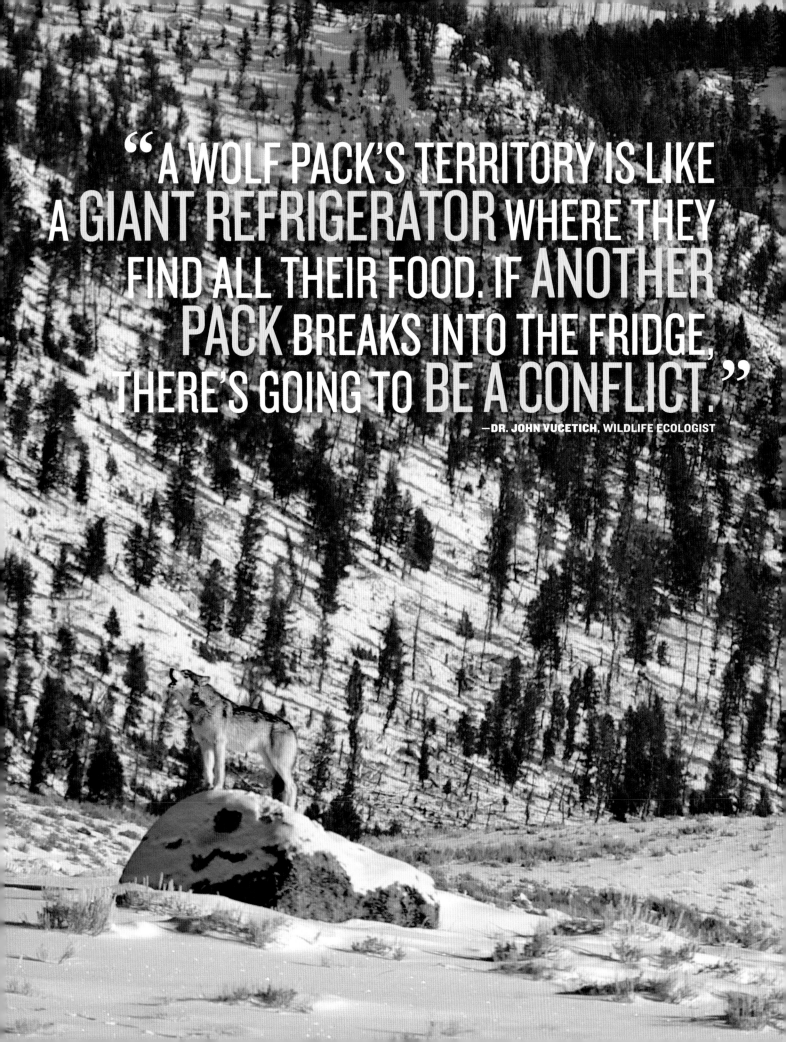

"A WOLF PACK'S TERRITORY IS LIKE A GIANT REFRIGERATOR WHERE THEY FIND ALL THEIR FOOD. IF ANOTHER PACK BREAKS INTO THE FRIDGE, THERE'S GOING TO BE A CONFLICT."

—DR. JOHN VUCETICH, WILDLIFE ECOLOGIST

For hundreds of thousands of years, wolves have roamed vast regions of the Earth. They have hidden in the mountain forests of North America and staked out homes in the extreme elevations of the Himalayan Mountains. They have survived desert heat and stayed warm in Arctic cold.

CANINE ORIGINS

Wolves likely originated in northern Europe and Asia and migrated to North America about 750,000 years ago. Wolves are what scientists refer to as generalists—they can occupy any temperate habitat (any area between the extreme climates of the North and South Poles). As long as there has been abundant prey, wolves have thrived in varied territories claimed in wild forests, mountains, tundra, and grasslands.

>> FAMILY TREE

Dogs have been man's best friend for more than 14,000 years, but all dogs, even wolves, descended from one common ancestor—*Leptocyon.*

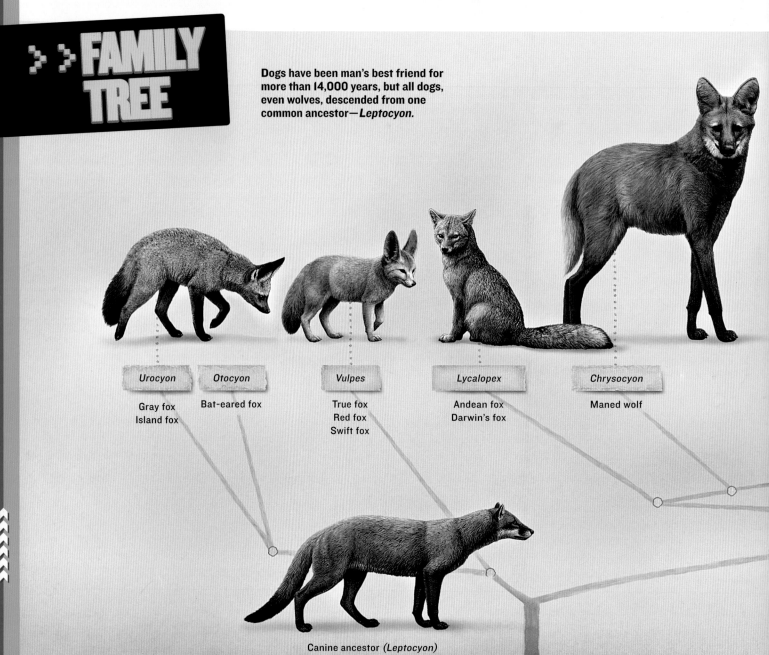

Urocyon	*Otocyon*	*Vulpes*	*Lycalopex*	*Chrysocyon*
Gray fox Island fox	Bat-eared fox	True fox Red fox Swift fox	Andean fox Darwin's fox	Maned wolf

Canine ancestor (*Leptocyon*)

There are three species of wolves: the gray wolf, the eastern wolf, and the critically endangered red wolf. And while few of the world's animal species are more studied than wolves, science remains unclear whether the eastern wolf is truly a separate species from the gray wolf. Scientists have debated this question for years, but Mother Nature still holds a few secrets. These days, most scientists agree on the two true wolf species, but there's plenty of wiggle room for different opinions.

WHO'S A WOLF AND WHO'S NOT

Wolves *(Canis lupus)* are part of the Canidae family. Currently recognized subspecies include the Mexican gray wolf *(Canis lupus baileyi)*, the northern timber wolf *(Canis lupus occidentalis)*, the Plains wolf *(Canis lupus nubilis)*, and the arctic wolf *(Canis lupus arctos)*.

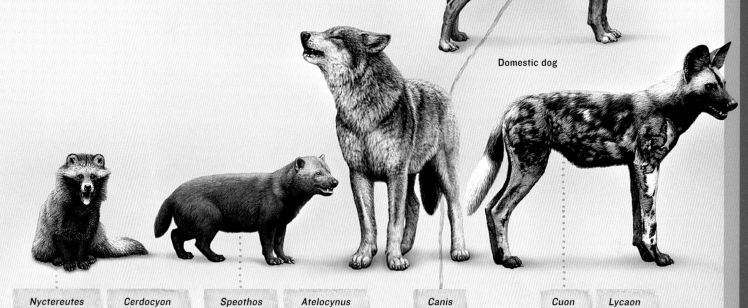

Domestic dog

Nyctereutes	Cerdocyon	Speothos	Atelocynus	Canis	Cuon	Lycaon
Raccoon dog	Common fox Crab-eating fox	Bush dog	Short-eared fox	Domestic dog Wolf Coyote Jackal	Asian wild dog Dhole	African wild dog

WOLF DETECTIVE

Like a detective in a murder investigation, if a wolf dies in Yellowstone National Park, Dr. Doug Smith figures out how and why, even if it means burrowing 12 feet (4 m) down into a snowdrift to find evidence. Dr. Smith has been in charge of the Yellowstone Gray Wolf Restoration Project in the park since the program's inception. To him, each wolf is an individual. He loves watching the different moods of nature, studying wolves' habits, and watching stories unfold, some of them over the course of years.

On a daily basis, Dr. Smith tracks radio-collared wolves by airplane, on foot, on skis, and on horseback. He has hand-raised wolf pups and supervises volunteers who work to protect Yellowstone wolves. He does research and writes about what he learns. He spends more time in his office than he'd like. But doing wolf-related work is a great way to connect with nature, even if it sometimes means working behind a desk instead of jumping out of a helicopter to put a radio collar on a

wolf or tracking a wolf through the park on his horse, Joker.

A student of the wolf since he was a kid, Dr. Smith read a lot about wolves and wrote letters to wolf biologists asking for advice. Intrigued by the predatory nature of wolves, he studied captive wolves at a sanctuary near his home and wrote a high school paper about his observations. Not long after that, a wolf biologist invited him to spend a summer researching wild wolves. He was hooked.

Dr. Smith believes that we all need to adopt the attitude that other animals besides humans are important, too. As an adult, he has devoted his career to researching and saving wolves. He hopes information based on his research will help people around the world understand and appreciate the value of preserving the lives of wolves.

Like arctic hares, polar bears, and even the bright white trumpeter swans, the arctic wolf's white coat provides excellent camouflage on the frozen tundra.

Scientists use these Latin names to identify and classify organisms. It's called "taxonomy." The names are identifiers, something like the name or number on the back of your soccer team shirt that identifies you. The scientific names can help us determine who's a wolf and who's not.

You've probably heard human beings referred to as *Homo sapiens.* That's our Latin name. "Homo" identifies the genus (or group) that we belong to. The second part refers to what species we're talking about.

For instance, your family's golden retriever *(Canis lupus familiaris)* is classified as a subspecies of the gray wolf. A third part of the scientific name identifies a subspecies, like *Canis lupus arctos,* the arctic wolf.

Other members of the canid group may be called wolf, but their scientific names reveal that these animals are actually not wolves. The Ethiopian wolf *(Canis simensis)* lacks "lupus" for a middle name, although the species shares many of the same struggles as true wolves. South America's maned wolf *(Chrysocyon brachyurus)* does too. But the maned wolf is not even part of the genus *Canis.* Here's a tricky one: The name of a wolverine sounds like a wolf. But the wolverine *(Gulo gulo)* belongs to the weasel family.

> **CLOSELY RELATED TO WOLVES, THE COYOTE'S SCIENTIFIC NAME IS *CANIS LATRANS.***

KINDS OF WOLVES

Wolves are pretty much the same no matter where they live. But a few distinct subspecies have geographic variants that make them different because of where they live, like the arctic wolf. They live along the northern edge of North America and northward to the North Pole, as well as along the eastern and northern shores of Greenland. Year-round white coats, slightly shorter noses, and smaller ears distinguish the arctic wolf from other gray wolf subspecies. Adaptations like thick fur and circulatory systems that keep their paws from freezing even in supercold temps help them survive.

The most endangered of all wolves, Mexican gray wolves—slightly smaller than other gray wolves—are also the most genetically distinct subspecies of wolf. That means their genetic coding is actually different

>> MEET A WOLF

RIO

The grandson of one of the last wild-caught Mexican gray wolves in existence, the wolf M166, also known as Rio, pioneered captive wolf breeding and reintroductions into the wild across the southwestern United States. Without him and his rare genetic code, Mexican wolves might have become extinct. In the early 1900s, the subspecies had been pretty much eliminated from Arizona, New Mexico, Texas, and south of the border in Mexico.

Born in captivity, Rio was one of the original 13 Mexican gray wolves released into the wild in 1998. Fit and bold, he was the first to take down natural prey and father a wild-born pup since his great-grandfather's days in the mountainous alpine forests of the southwestern United States.

Rio's contribution to the return of the Mexican wolf to the wild made him a star. He had a fan club and was the subject of profiles in newspapers and magazines. But life is never easy for a wolf. His first mate in the wild was shot. A mountain lion killed his second mate. His next three female partners had a dangerous taste for cattle. After a series of livestock kills, he and his last mate were retired to a secluded home at the California Wolf Center in southern California. Even after Rio's death at the remarkable age of 15, his contributions live on.

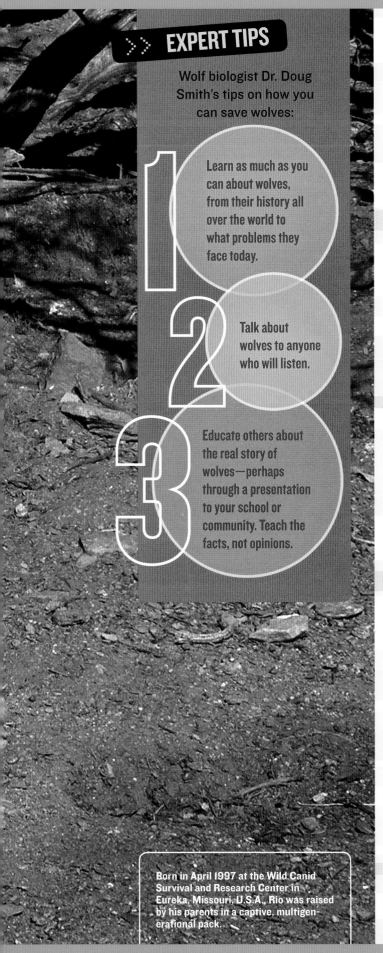

Wolf biologist Dr. Doug Smith's tips on how you can save wolves:

1 Learn as much as you can about wolves, from their history all over the world to what problems they face today.

2 Talk about wolves to anyone who will listen.

3 Educate others about the real story of wolves—perhaps through a presentation to your school or community. Teach the facts, not opinions.

Born in April 1997 at the Wild Canid Survival and Research Center in Eureka, Missouri, U.S.A., Rio was raised by his parents in a captive, multigenerational pack.

from other wolves. Scientists love to debate what that means. Historically, Mexican gray wolves have lived throughout the southeastern United States and Mexico.

DO NOT ENTER

A wolf's territory is simply where his pack lives and hunts. The family structure, or pack, is very possessive of the land they live on and very competitive with their neighbors. Minnesota wolves "protect" their prey populations of deer. In Yellowstone National Park, wolves get territorial about elk. Arctic wolves hunt musk oxen, Peary caribou, and arctic hares on vast territories that may cover as much as 1,000 square miles (2,590 sq km).

Physical attacks are one way wolves advertise territorial boundaries. They also scent-mark their territories with urine or traces of secretions from scent glands like the ones found in the webs of the paws. Howling is another way wolves tell other wolves to keep out.

Wolves often invade other territories in hopes of expanding their own boundaries. How well a pack can defend its territory or take over another's depends on pack size and muscle. A pack of 4 wolves has little chance against an invading pack that's 17 wolves strong.

HUMAN INVADERS

But there's little that wolves can do about humans invading wolf territory. Perhaps humans are just as territorial as wolves or even more. As we have encroached on wolves' territories, conflicts with these shy creatures have increased. Battles over land and food (which still go on today) rarely end in a wolf's favor. These animals are very resilient, but there is a limit to how long their populations can survive without cooperation from humans. Wolves' success in many cases has depended on whether they could reproduce faster than humans could kill them.

By the late 1920s in the United States, gray wolves had been wiped out from north to south. Only wolves in Alaska, northeast Minnesota, and Isle Royale, Michigan, survived. Today they are one of the most abundant types of wolves in the world because of their limited exposure to humans.

Mexican gray wolves, nicknamed "lobo" (the Spanish word for wolf), have a long history of run-ins with humans in their territory. Large-scale trapping and poisoning of wolves in the early 1900s caused their disappearance. Wolves like Rio, who you met on page 36, helped bring Mexican gray wolves back.

There are only about 75 Mexican gray wolves alive in the wild today. Fragile populations have been rebuilt through breeding and reintroduction programs at zoos in Mexico and the United States. In the U.S., successful breeding and reintroduction programs have brought lobos back to National Forest lands in Arizona and New Mexico, but there are no wild wolves roaming Mexico today.

Red wolves were hunted to near extinction in the 1960s, primarily by farmers protecting their livestock. Similar stories played out in Europe and Asia.

Wolves have two requirements for creating territories. First, they must have access to enough prey. Second, they need tolerance from human beings.

>> WOLF SPOTLIGHT
YOUR DOG'S RELATIVE

Today's dogs most likely evolved from wolves. Dogs and wolves use much of the same body language to communicate with their families.

Wagging tail, lowered chest, and a rump in the air means: "Let's play!"

Licks are an unthreatening, happy greeting that means: "I'm happy to see you."

An open mouth and tense body means: "Back off!"

Ears up, tail upright, and chest held high means: "Let's go!"

Wolves, like this Mexican gray, can trot for miles, searching for prey and patrolling the pack's territory at the same time.

TO MARK HIS TERRITORY, A BREEDING WOLF WILL SCRATCH THE GROUND WITH HIS PAW, LEAVING A SMELLY SCRATCH-AND-SNIFF MESSAGE FOR ANOTHER WOLF.

These red wolf pups, in a litter of six born in a captive breeding facility of Tacoma, Washington, U.S.A.'s Point Defiance Zoo, stop and listen to a new noise—the clicking of a camera.

If people poison, shoot, and trap wolves, populations are not likely to succeed. Water is a secondary concern. The wolf is something of an all-terrain vehicle. As long as it has fuel and tough treads, it can go anywhere.

CHANGE

In southern Europe, as government agencies and conservation groups have collaborated to save wolves, populations have recolonized in countries like France and Italy. In many regions of Europe, wolves carve out a healthy existence despite living in landscapes dominated by humans. They live in cornfields in Spain. They make dens in garbage cans on the edge of cities in Croatia and Israel, staying out of sight during the day and scavenging for trash all over town at night. In Italy, they survive on humans' leftovers at trash dumps on the outskirts of Rome.

In the United States, the Endangered Species Act

DYNAMIC DENS!

A wolf's den might be in a cave, a deep hole dug at the base of a fir tree, in a hollow log, or in an old beaver lodge.

of 1973 provided protection for wolves. Around that time, even though red wolf populations had essentially been wiped out, scientists found a small population of red wolves along the Gulf Coast of Texas and Louisiana. Biologists captured as many of these priceless red wolves as possible—17 individuals—14 of whom became the foundation of a successful breeding program. Enough red wolves have been bred in captivity to reintroduce them in wildlife refuges in North Carolina, where a wild population remains today.

Major reintroduction projects, like the reintroduction of gray wolves into Yellowstone National Park in 1995 and 1996 from wild packs in Canada and the ongoing reintroduction of Mexican gray wolves in the southwestern United States, have enabled wild

A WOLF PACK'S TERRITORY CAN BE AS SMALL AS 15 SQUARE MILES (38.8 SQ KM) OR AS LARGE AS 2,500 SQUARE MILES (6,475 SQ KM), DEPENDING ON WHERE IT LIVES.

populations to rebound. Increasing tolerance of wolves in Europe and parts of Asia has done the same.

Today, wolf populations have increased all over the world, particularly in North America, Europe, and Asia, which has a wide range of wolf territory. Despite encroachment from humans on wolves' habitat, wild wolves can be found living in regions from southern Alaska to the mountains of Italy. In Canada, wolf territory extends from east to west. In the United States, they live in Minnesota, Wisconsin, Oregon, Michigan, Idaho, Montana, Washington, Arizona, and New Mexico. Red wolves can be found in wildlife refuges in North Carolina. Wolves stake out territories throughout a gigantic block of land from far eastern Siberia down into Mongolia and China and all the way west to Finland.

It's the species' ability to survive that gives wolves their incredible global distribution: They do well almost anywhere. Do you know someone who has moved around a lot? Perhaps that person's like a wolf: tough and adaptable.

Wolves' overall recovery has been so successful that in the Rocky Mountains and Great Lakes areas of the U.S., gray wolves are no longer listed by the federal government as an endangered species. Now, individual states manage their wolf populations like they manage wild bears, deer, and moose to maintain sustainable numbers of wild animals. But it's not a perfect system.

In the United States, and around the world, many different views exist about how to manage wild animals. The fact that wolves often eat the same food as humans makes it hard for wolves to compete. In states where wild wolves roam near cattle ranches and sheep farms, ranchers fear that wolves will kill their livestock. In states like Wyoming and Montana, where hunting is a tradition and how people feed their families (not unlike wolves themselves), many people believe wolves take more than their fair share of elk and deer and wish they hadn't been reintroduced.

On the other hand, animal protection activists hope to save every single wolf. Average tourists are much more likely to have the thrill of seeing a wild wolf on a trek through the park. Conservationists celebrate the return of wolves.

>> ANIMAL RESCUE!

ENDANGERED SPECIES ACT   ‹‹‹

Without a protective law called the Endangered Species Act, gray wolves in the northern Rockies, grizzly bears, bald eagles, and even the petite Miami blue butterfly might have vanished by now. But in 1973, the United States Congress passed legislation that recognized the country's rich wild landscape and vowed to save it.

It's a good thing. After decades of wolf-killing by poisoning, trapping, and shooting, there were only a few hundred beautiful wolves left in the lower 48 of the United States.

After the law passed, it was illegal to capture, harm, or kill a wolf. Free of persecution (and not required to show a passport or travel through border patrol), wolves dispersed on foot from Canada to create new packs in northwest Montana. In the mid-1990s, 66 Canadian wolves were reintroduced into Yellowstone National Park and central Idaho. Wolves thrived, thanks to the protections provided by the Endangered Species Act.

Today, thousands of wolves live in Minnesota and western states like Montana, Wyoming, and Idaho. They have even reached California, Oregon, and Washington. In 2012, gray wolves in the northern Rocky Mountains were delisted, or removed from the list of federally endangered animals. Now, as they do with any other wildlife, the national parks and states manage their own thriving wolf populations.

>> RESCUE ACTIVITIES

NOVICE

MAPPING CANIDS

Canids are a family of animals that include wolves, dogs, foxes, and jackals. Even if you don't have wolves in your neighborhood, you will almost certainly have dogs that share many characteristics and behaviors of their wolf relatives. Just like a scientist exploring the geography of canids in the wild, this challenge is all about mapping our canine friends.

MAPPING WOLF IMAGES

WOLVES OFTEN APPEAR IN LOGOS, symbols, statues, and crests. This is because they are seen as symbols of mystery, beauty, and power. How many can you find where you live?

GO ONLINE TO CHECK OUT OTHER BUSINESSES THAT INCORPORATE WOLVES INTO THEIR LOGO. If it's not clear from their company information, write a letter asking what they do to help wolves as part of their business plan.

TAKE UP A WOLF DONATION. Can you persuade a company that uses a wolf in its logo to start giving a regular donation to a wolf rescue charity?

MAPPING CANID CONFLICT AND KINDNESS

PEOPLE, PROPERTY, DOGS, FOXES, WILDLIFE, AND FARMED ANIMALS DO NOT ALWAYS GET ALONG. Explore your local area again, but this time look especially for signs of conflict or kindness.

EXTREME

ADVANCED

MAPPING DOG ACTIVITY

CREATE A DOG ACTIVITY MAP for your local area by printing or drawing a map of your local area. Make it as big as you can.

MARK YOUR TERRITORY LIMITS onto the map and get permission to explore your territory looking for evidence of canids. You might be able to roam farther if you take an adult with you.

ADD YOUR DISCOVERIES to your map. Make sure you record the different kinds of dogs that you find and any evidence, including bones and dog poop. Can you photograph a dog that looks just like a wolf?

INVESTIGATE YOUR FINDINGS. What do they reveal? Are some parts of the neighborhood more dog-friendly than others? What kinds of canids live in your area?

To do this challenge, you'll learn all about maps. Here are some tips to do this challenge successfully:

1

Many wolves will walk 30 miles (48 km) of territory in a single day. So remember to think big!

2

An accurate map is important since our towns and neighborhoods are changing every day. Check with your local library to see if they have the latest and greatest maps of your town or city.

3

Study your map before you head out on your expedition. Have a big territory to cover? Take friends, an adult or two, and divide and conquer.

ON YOUR MAP, MARK IN RED: mean barking, nasty growling, aggressive snapping, and biting. Make sure you stay far away if you encounter any of these behaviors. Animal aggression may also be recorded in your local police department's log. **MARK IN GREEN:** friendly barking, playing, friendly rolling around, and bottom sniffing.

DOES YOUR GEOGRAPHIC RESEARCH REVEAL ANY PATTERNS? Is there more canid conflict in some places than others? Share your map with your local community. Suggest ways to shrink the red conflict areas and expand green peaceful areas.

CHAPTER 3

>> ALL IN THE FAMILY

A pack of gray wolves might be on the move for up to eight hours a day as they search for prey.

"FOR THE STRENGTH OF THE PACK IS THE WOLF AND THE STRENGTH OF THE WOLF IS THE PACK."

THE JUNGLE BOOK BY RUDYARD KIPLING

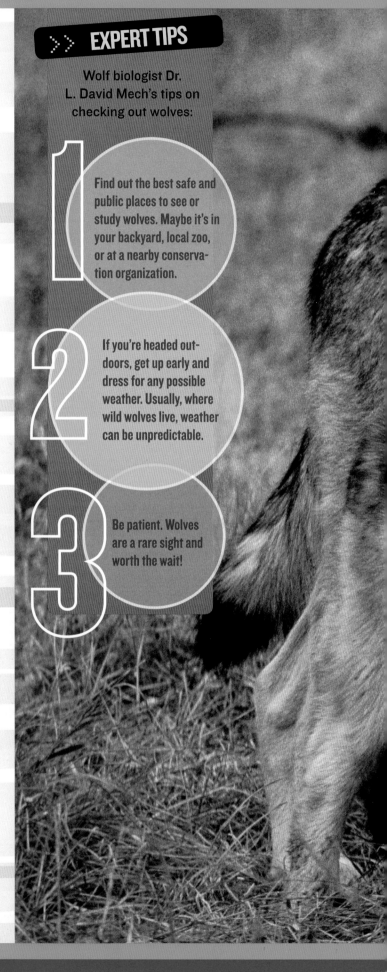

amily meals, road trips, chores: Your family has more in common with a pack of wolves than you might think. Does your aunt ever babysit you and your siblings? Do your parents work together to support the family and bring home food? Like a human family, wolf packs are made up of parents, their offspring, and sometimes aunts, uncles, and cousins—most related, some not. Members of a wolf pack take care of each other, eat together, hunt together, defend their territory together, and sometimes have disagreements.

THE WAY OF THE WOLF

Human pack or wolf pack, rules help keep order. And like your parents make the rules in your family, the top wolves—the mother and father wolf—make the rules for how a wolf pack operates. It's their job to keep everyone safe, fed, and to maintain order in the group. They are also usually the only breeding pair in a group.

Many scientists consider the term "alpha wolf" to be outdated. It implies that the lead wolf earned his rank through fighting. What really happens is that the breeding male and female in a wild pack produce offspring. As parents, they become the natural leaders of the group, like in a human family. While competition for dominance might occur when members of a captive wolf pack assembled by humans figure out their hierarchy, that rarely happens in the wild.

Lone wolves are often wolves that have dispersed, or left their packs to find a mate. Temporarily alone, they face hardships that wolves in a pack do not. A healthy wolf can bring down an old or injured elk on

DEPENDING ON THE CONTEXT, A WOLF'S GROWL CAN BE A WARNING OR AN INVITATION TO PLAY.

>> **EXPERT TIPS**

Wolf biologist Dr. L. David Mech's tips on checking out wolves:

1 Find out the best safe and public places to see or study wolves. Maybe it's in your backyard, local zoo, or at a nearby conservation organization.

2 If you're headed outdoors, get up early and dress for any possible weather. Usually, where wild wolves live, weather can be unpredictable.

3 Be patient. Wolves are a rare sight and worth the wait!

Eating can be a messy affair for wolves, like this juvenile female gray wolf and her father.

THE INTERNATIONAL WOLF CENTER

Ely, Minnesota, U.S.A., is home to wolves and wolf lovers. For more than 70 years, wolf research in the area has contributed to the understanding of wolves. The area is also home to a thriving wild population.

In 1985, Dr. L. David Mech, who you will read about on pages 56 and 57, launched a committee to create the facility as an extension of his research about wolves. He also wanted to help people around the world better understand, and help save, wolves.

The International Wolf Center, a global center for research and information about wolves, is also in Ely, at the edge of the Boundary Waters Canoe Wilderness Area. The building's triangular windows suggest wolf eyes and ears. Observation windows look into a 1.25-acre (0.5 hectare) wolf enclosure and den site, home for the resident wolf pack.

his own, but a team helps. Wolves on their own often scavenge other kills or settle for easier-to-kill prey such as birds, beavers, and mice—a very small meal compared to what a typical pack feasts on after a kill. Wherever they wander, lone wolves have to be wary: They risk a vicious attack if they enter another wolf pack's territory. Wolves have strong family ties but they aren't welcoming neighbors.

Within a group, wolves maintain roles and relationships they might keep their whole lives. In addition to the breeding wolves, a pack might have mid-ranking adult wolves (all with their own personalities and quirks) who fall into a natural hierarchy. This order determines who breeds, who eats first, who sleeps where, where they hunt, and who babysits the pups. Rank doesn't have to do with a wolf's size but rather personality. The largest wolf in the pack, for instance, could end up as the lowest ranking member if he's a quiet observer, a class clown, or an obedient follower.

In Idaho's Sawtooth Pack, made famous by wildlife photographers and filmmakers Jim and Jamie Dutcher, the biggest wolf in the pack, Lakota, was also the lowest ranking. Lakota's brother Kamots became the breeding male in the group. Both were beautiful gray wolves with black and white markings. Where his brother was a feisty, brave explorer, timid Lakota followed his brother rather than exploring on his own. He often appeared to crouch, perhaps trying to make his large body seem small.

But even low-ranking Lakota had an important job: remain submissive (always giving way to others) and instigate play to keep everyone in the pack in a good mood. Being the lowest ranked member is a job, and

Like humans, wolves have families, work to do, lessons to learn, and places to go.

someone's got to do it. The Dutchers, in their close observation of life within a wolf pack, believe the role of this submissive wolf helped to alleviate pack tension. He was also forced to eat last and was the focus of pack aggression, yet he was a very important member of the pack.

SAFETY IN NUMBERS

Like any good team, a wolf pack relies on clear communication. Wolves are a lot like kids; they can express themselves in many different ways. You can talk, yell, whine, whistle, wave your hands, stomp your feet, or give someone a funny look to get your point across. Wolves can too—well, almost. Instead, a wolf might howl, whine, whimper, snarl, growl, squeak, yelp, yip, flatten his ears, curl his lip (this behavior even has a name; it's called an agnostic pucker), or swat another member of his pack with his paw to get his message across. One thing wolves don't often do: bark.

People and wolves can say a lot without words. From head to tail, a wolf expresses information through subtle and obvious body language. Facial expressions and how a wolf holds his tail express

IF A WOLF NEEDS TO WHISPER, HE MIGHT USE A SOFT _WOOF_.

confidence or submission to another wolf. The higher a wolf ranks in the pack, the higher he stands and holds his head, ears, and tail. The lower he ranks, the smaller he tries to be, crouching, crawling, tucking, flopping, and rolling over on his back exposing his vulnerable belly as a sign of surrender.

Lower ranking wolves lick the muzzles of their parents and older siblings to show they know who's boss. Happy wolves wag their tails and stretch down in playful bows like domestic dogs. But if play gets out of hand, the breeding male or female—like the teacher on the playground—can straighten out unruliness with a warning glare. One cold stare might be all it takes for a wolf to straighten out a subordinate. But pack leaders get tough if they have to. Narrowed eyes, bared fangs, and a low growl are a serious warning.

Since a wolf can't text his pack mates about his whereabouts, when he'll be home, or update the status of elk via social media, he has to rely on sound and smell as his main communication tools. Vocal communications indicate how a wolf is feeling or what he's about to do. Scent messages give a picture of his history and status.

ANIMAL SUPERPOWERS   WOLF SPEAK

WOLVES HOWL TO KEEP COMPETING PACKS OUT OF THEIR TERRITORY AND TO STAY IN TOUCH WITH MEMBERS OF THEIR OWN PACK.

WOLVES CAN TELL BY LISTENING TO ANOTHER WOLF'S HOWL IF IT IS PREPARING TO HUNT OR READY TO MATE.

A WOLF CAN EVEN TELL IF ANOTHER WOLF IS A FRIEND OR FOE . . .

AND IF IT'S IN A GOOD MOOD OR NOT . . .

JUST BY LISTENING TO ITS HOWL.

>> MEET A WOLF

BRUTUS

At the first twilight in four months on northern Canada's Ellesmere Island, the February sun finally rises after a cold, dark winter. A large, imposing arctic wolf named Brutus leads his pack on the hunt. Maybe they'll take down a huge, furry musk ox grazing on the frozen, windswept grassland. Maybe Brutus will have to make do with an arctic hare.

Wild and snow-white, Brutus led his pack for years on the remote island, 600 miles (965 km) from the North Pole. Dr. L. David Mech, who has studied wolves close-up for decades, tracked Brutus for many of those years, camping outside the wolf's den and observing him summer after summer. Arctic wolves have had limited exposure to humans and are not as afraid as other wild wolves. Once the wild wolf got so close as to sniff Dr. Mech's glove. Wearing a radio collar around his neck, Brutus taught Dr. Mech about wolves even after the scientist left the island at the end of each summer. The collar transmitted information to a satellite. The system emailed Dr. Mech every day about Brutus's location.

By the time Brutus died at ten years old—a lengthy life for a wild wolf— he had provided scientists a tremendous amount of new information about where arctic wolves travel throughout the year and what they eat. As a tribute to his work, today Brutus's body stands (mounted by taxidermy) immortalized at the Eureka Weather Station on Ellesmere Island.

WOLF COLORS

Most wolf pups are born with blue eyes, which usually change to yellow.

Wolves have powerful noses. These adult male gray wolves investigate a scent in Idaho's Sawtooth Mountains.

A WOLF SPENDS ALMOST 24 HOURS A DAY WITH HIS PACK, DIVIDING HIS TIME EQUALLY BETWEEN SLEEPING, SOCIALIZING, AND PATROLLING HIS TERRITORY.

Heard up to 5 miles (8 km) away through the forest or 10 miles (16 km) away on the tundra, a wolf howls to call members together, warn of danger, remind neighboring packs to stay out of his territory, or just for joy.

A wolf's "sniff channel" (we're talking about his nose) gives him a serious ability to receive messages through smell. A wolf's sense of smell is about a hundred times more sensitive than that of us humans. And he can *leave* a trail of scents through his urine and secretions left behind from the many scent glands on his body, like the ones on the pads of his paws.

Through the scents that he leaves, a wolf transmits information about his identity, age, gender, and social status. It's a three-dimensional world of odors, almost impossible for a human to comprehend.

Like members of a human family, young wolves in the pack grow up and set out on their own. Once a wolf reaches 18 months or two years old—college age in human years—a wolf usually leaves its pack to find a mate. Some move next door, some move long distances. Once a new breeding pair has found each other, they will stake out a territory and hopefully produce a litter of four to six pups each year, establishing a new pack.

PUPPY LOVE

At birth, a wolf pup—who can't see, smell much, or hear yet—weighs only about a pound (453 g). That's like a can of soda. But wolf pups don't stay small for long. The pups gorge themselves on Mom's nutritious milk. After snuggling in the den with her for the first two weeks or so, their eyes open and they begin to crawl. Their protector and their food source, Mom hardly leaves the den. Other pack members bring her meat. At just two weeks old, the tiny pups chew on bits of flesh for the first time with their sharp teeth.

At three weeks they wander out of the den into the sunlight for the first time and meet the rest of the pack. Now they are explorers! At just five weeks old, they begin to wean themselves and can travel with the pack on trips up to about a mile (1.6 km) long.

I was part of a large team of biologists who helped restore wolves to Yellowstone National Park. My own role included writing, testifying in Congress and court, consulting and advising, as well as assisting with organizing the capture, handling, and release of the wolves.

Howling is a learning experience! This gray wolf mom teaches her pups how to howl in the Montana forest.

DR. L. DAVID MECH

BORN: AUBURN, NEW YORK, U.S.A.
JOB TITLE: SENIOR RESEARCH SCIENTIST
AFFILIATION: U.S. GEOLOGICAL SURVEY
JOB LOCATIONS: ST. PAUL, MINNESOTA, U.S.A.;
SUPERIOR NATIONAL FOREST; AND YELLOWSTONE
NATIONAL PARK
YEARS WORKING WITH WOLVES: 55
MONTHS A YEAR IN THE FIELD: 1–4

How are you helping to save wolves?
Learning about them and how they live so government agencies managing them have the best information to base their decisions on.

Favorite thing about your job?
Being out in the field working with wolves, observing them, catching them, collaring them, and tracking them. I learn all I can about wolves, how they live, behave, and interact with other species, especially with their prey and with humans.

Best thing about working in the field?
I have studied wolves in Minnesota, Canada, Italy, Alaska, Yellowstone National Park, and other places where wild wolves live. I like intimately interacting with the natural world and being part of it. Once, an arctic wolf pup playfully untied my bootlace.

Worst thing about working in the field?
Having to leave. Also bad weather can be a problem.

How can kids prepare to do your job one day?
Take many science and math courses in school and college. Study hard. Get as much experience as you can hiking, camping, skiing, canoeing, fishing, and hunting.

READY! SET! ACTION!

Documentary producer and camera-man Bob Landis grew up trophy hunting deer, elk, and wild sheep with his father with both a gun and a camera. His fascination with wolves ignited on a trip to Alaska's Denali National Park when he was 25 years old. It was his wife Connie's insistence that they go on that trip that changed their lives. These days, their home in Montana shares a property line with Yellowstone National Park.

Over the years, Landis's fascination with wildlife has shifted from hunting into shooting wildlife with a camera. When it comes to wolves, he's helping save them by educating the public through a camera lens, illustrating the lives of wolves by capturing unique sequences of behaviors on film.

Landis has made five documentaries about wolves for National Geographic Television, including a 2014 film about the famous '06 Female you read about on page 19. He's also made wildlife films about coyotes and bears.

Landis spends 12 months a year in the field. He even goes out on the coldest days of the year. His camera still works at minus 40°F (−40°C), though the batteries (and his fingers) don't work as well as usual.

Denning season for wolves starts with the birth of pups, usually in the spring.

By 12 to 16 weeks old, the pups weigh 20 times what they did at birth. Since the pups are no longer limited to the den, the pack has more freedom to move around. Toward the end of the spring, they move to what's called a rendezvous (or get-together) site where the pack spends a lot of time. It's where the pups wait—perhaps with a babysitter wolf—while the pack hunts until they are old enough to travel with the pack full-time.

Although a curious pup will often chew sticks and gobble berries, Mom never says, "Eat your vegetables." When pack members return from a successful hunt, pups lick up at the lips of the adult wolves. This causes them to regurgitate chewed meat, which the pups snarf up. This might seem disgusting to you, but to a wolf pup it's like having a pizza delivered.

When a pup is about four months old, he might stalk real prey like rabbits and mice. At six months old, the pups are old enough to join the hunt. Inexperienced and trailing behind, sometimes the newbies' lack of skill messes up the hunt. But it's how they learn.

SCHOOL FOR PUPS

Do you like to play hide-and-seek or tag? So do wolf pups. Playing with their littermates and older brothers and sisters helps them to learn important survival lessons for when they're adults. They stalk, leap, pounce, chase, wrestle, and grab on to each other's soft ears in pretend hunts.

They also play with toys—but not tennis balls and rubber bones from the pet store like their domestic cousins. No, these pups ravage animal skins from a kill, bones and feathers—killing their "prey" over and over again and parading them around like trophies.

Other wolves in the pack—their older siblings, aunts, and uncles—are often lighthearted jungle gyms for the playful pups. Pups bite the adults' tails, paws, ears, and anything they can grab in their spiky teeth. Sometimes if they're lucky, an adult brings them a chunk of meat to gnaw on.

They learn other lessons, too—how to interact and communicate with each other, the subtleties of aggression, and defending themselves against other wolves are skills the pups will use later in life to chase other wolves out of their territory, a key requirement for the pack's survival.

>>RESCUE ACTIVITIES

WOLF GAMES

Saving wolves is a serious business, but often fun is the best way to motivate other people to do good things. Playing games like a wolf pup can be a way to bring a pack of people together and help to save wolves. This challenge is all about designing a wolf-like game. Play it and in the process raise awareness of some of the problems that wolves face.

Invent your game by picking wolf-like objectives, rules, and players from each of these lists.

NOVICE

BASIC GAME PLAY

COME UP WITH THE AIM OF YOUR GAME. Wolves always have an agenda, so should you! Pick one or more objectives. Some sample objectives could be: capturing prey, defending territory, or evading capture.

EVEN IN THE WILD, IT'S ALL ABOUT COMPETITION. Play against others in your pack or find another pack to compete against. You could compete against lone wolves, small packs of 2–6 wolves, medium packs of 7–14 wolves, or large packs of 15 or more wolves.

SET UP YOUR WOLF RULES. Some examples are stay inside your territory; communicate only by howling, whining, whimpering, and making other wolf sounds; always move on all fours; and no actual biting or scratching.

EXTREME

SHOWING OFF

MAKE YOUR GAME MORE EXTREME WITH A TWIST. Use the game as an event to help your audience understand how they can help save wolves.

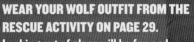

Rules:

GETTING COMPETITIVE

CREATE A RULE BOOK that explains how to play your game. Include some facts and information about wolves that will help players to learn about them. Hand it out not just to the players, but to the audience, too!

WEAR YOUR WOLF OUTFIT FROM THE RESCUE ACTIVITY ON PAGE 29. Looking out of place will be fun and help raise awareness for what you are doing.

ORGANIZE A COMPETITION AT SCHOOL—or between schools! Get teachers, parents, and after-school organizations to help you plan a school-wide event.

All games including professional sports and wolf pups playing with their parents include rules, even if they are unspoken. Here are some tips and thinking that will help you make your game inventing even better:

1 Add another layer to your game with luck. Use a coin, dice, or a spinner to randomize a rule or to enact new rules during play!

2 A successful game needs a time limit and space limit or it could get out of hand. Plan these out before you start and make sure to clearly label boundaries.

3 Objects add another level of complexity to your game. Try balls, flags, or objects in nature to make your game tougher.

CREATE AN ONLINE BLOG to showcase pictures, video, and create buzz for the event. Contact your local newspaper or TV station and ask if they will cover the event.

PLAY IN A VERY LARGE AREA and include a large number of players. The biggest wolf packs can include over 35 individuals. The bigger you get the louder your howl! Ask all players to give a donation to a wolf conservation charity.

CHAPTER 4

>>> ON THE HUNT

" THE WOLF'S PREDATOR LIFESTYLE IS A FEAST-OR-FAMINE EXISTENCE. "
—DR. L. DAVID MECH, WOLF BIOLOGIST

When a wolf curls his lip back to show his teeth, shows a hard stare, and flattens his ears to the side, like this captive wolf eating a deer carcass, it means "stay back!"

A wolf's winter coat is made up of a top layer of guard fur and a thick undercoat. This lone gray wolf moves quickly in pursuit of a meal.

Hunger. Days of hunger. A wolf feels the empty ache just about all the time. Feast or famine: It's a constant of the predator lifestyle. Brave and adventurous travelers, packs of agile, sure-footed wolves cover long distances—sometimes 30 miles (48 km) in a day—searching out their prey and hunting it down.

DEADLY DINNER

The point of hunting, of course, is to eat. But hunting can be deadly for a wolf, too. Territory disputes with competing packs while a wolf searches for prey, a blow from the hoof of a moose struggling to survive, a mortal stab from a bison's horn, or a tangle with a grizzly bear can all mean death for a wolf—and increase the chances of his pack going hungry.

Imagine a pack of wolves walking for miles to search for prey like elk, moose, deer, or bison (usually the old or sick) or easier-to-catch small prey like beaver, rabbits, rodents, and even salmon in Alaska, U.S.A., or coastal British Columbia, Canada. His nose twitches when his large black nostrils detect the scent of an old moose. His long legs pick up speed. Still, it's a while before he actually sees the 900-pound (408 kg) meal. It's ten times his size, but hunger wins out over fear.

He launches an attack from behind. Striking with his inch-long (2.5 cm) fangs, he clamps down with his powerful jaws and interlocking teeth. The moose runs, dragging the wolf through the forest. The pack surrounds the moose. It finally gives in and they finish the job. The wolves settle in for their first meal in a week. They gorge themselves, consuming as much as 20 pounds (9 kg) of meat each—about the same amount as 460 chicken nuggets—in one meal. Have you ever wondered where that saying "wolfing your food" came from? Now you know.

ONE TOUGH CUSTOMER

What if you had to take down a cow with your teeth just to eat a hamburger for dinner tonight? Wolves have a very different relationship with their food

TALK TO THE PAW

Wolves are digitigrade, which means they walk and run on their toes for increased agility and speed—up to 36–38 miles an hour (58–61 km/h) in short bursts.

Front paws can be more than 5 inches (12.7 cm) long and 4 inches (10.2 cm) wide.

Tough, calloused toe pads spread out on the snow, distributing weight as if they were snowshoes.

Tufts of coarse hair insulate each toe and improve grip on ice, rocks, and steep terrain.

Toes stick together when walking on easy terrain, but stretch apart or flex up and down—to grasp rough surfaces and balance.

>> MEET A WOLF
THE DIRE WOLF

For tens of thousands of years, oil has seeped up through the Earth's crust in the western United States. The result is black tar deposits that—especially during the Ice Age—were thick enough to trap animals. And trap the predators that tried to eat the trapped animals. It's a sticky subject.

Today, one such area is called the La Brea Tar Pits in Los Angeles, California. Scientists and archaeologists have excavated more than a million bones from deep inside the pits including more than 4,000 dire wolves *(Canis dirus)*, more than 2,000 individual saber-toothed cats and almost as many coyotes, plus bones from 228 other vertebrates.

This massive Ice Age wolf—the largest canid that ever existed—roamed a huge range from the grasslands of South America all the way up to the glaciers of North America. Remains of the 300,000-year-old dire wolf can be found all over America. But they're especially common on the East Coast of the United States in Florida north to Pennsylvania and also in California and Oregon.

The dire wolf's head and teeth were bigger than the modern-day wolf's. Thicker, shorter legs suggest they were slower, too. They could grow to 150 pounds (68 kg) and lived alongside creatures like the saber-toothed tiger. Some scientists believe that humans may have indirectly caused the disappearance of this massive Ice Age wolf. Human predators may have hunted the herbivores (grass-eating mammals that the dire wolf relied on for food) to extinction about 8,000 years ago, leaving the dire wolf without a food source.

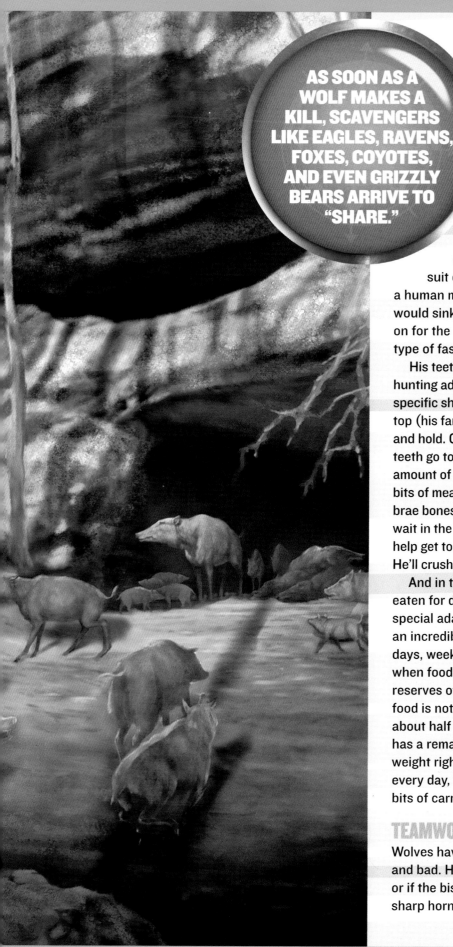

AS SOON AS A WOLF MAKES A KILL, SCAVENGERS LIKE EAGLES, RAVENS, FOXES, COYOTES, AND EVEN GRIZZLY BEARS ARRIVE TO "SHARE."

than humans do, especially those of us who are used to buying our food at the grocery store. A wolf's life is not easy, especially when it comes to feeding himself and the pack. But his body is designed for hunting—those adaptations are his best defense against hunger.

One of his most important hunting adaptations is his ability to be tough. In pursuit of food, a wolf endures pain and abuse that a human might not survive. Who else do you know that would sink his teeth into the rear of a moose and hang on for the ride, just for a meal? It's a whole different type of fast food—hold the fries.

His teeth are another one of the wolf's most obvious hunting adaptations. Each of his 42 pearly whites has a specific shape and purpose. The canine teeth—two on top (his fangs) and two on the bottom—puncture, rip, and hold. Once the kill is on the ground, the incisor teeth go to work helping the wolf get the greatest amount of food possible. The incisors nibble and grab bits of meat from tiny crevices, like around the vertebrae bones of an elk. The carnassial teeth, or molars, wait in the back of his enormously powerful jaws. They help get to the fatty, nutrient-rich marrow inside bones. He'll crush and eat the bones later if food is scarce.

And in those periods of time when a wolf hasn't eaten for days or weeks, a wolf's digestive system has special adaptations to keep him from starving. He has an incredible capacity to fast, or to go without food for days, weeks, and even months. During periods of time when food is scarce, a wolf's body first uses all his reserves of fat. As long as water is available, a lack of food is not life-threatening to a wolf until he's lost about half of his body weight. Once he eats again, he has a remarkable ability to store food and gain the weight right back. Of course, a wolf would love to eat every day, but he can survive on bones and occasional bits of carrion (other predators' leftovers) for months.

TEAMWORK

Wolves have good days (when hunting is successful) and bad. Hunger can last for days if the elk gets away or if the bison stands his ground, threatening with sharp horns. Even with all of the adaptations that help

them hunt, wolves have their weaknesses, too. They're nothing like the superpredator wolves portrayed in the Twilight movies.

WOLF WEAKNESSES

Think about it this way: Compared to lions, wolves don't have a lot of specialized killing equipment. An African lion has 2.5-inch (6.35 cm) fangs (compared to a wolf's I-inch [2.5 cm] fangs). A lion's retractable claws can grab and pull down huge prey practically out of the air, whereas a wolf's claws aren't designed to pierce or grab. A lion's jaws can kill an antelope with a single bite. A wolf doesn't have that kind of power. His fangs are too far from the hinge where the muscle connects to the jaw (it's like grabbing a pair of pliers farther back; you can't squeeze them as tightly the farther back you go). The lion also has loose belly skin that protects from kicks or jabs of an antler. That's an insurance policy a wolf doesn't have.

But, while most carnivores—from tigers right on down to weasels—live solitary lives, one thing wolves have is each other. Even though a healthy adult wolf can take down prey alone, they are most effective hunting in groups of four or five. Scientists in Yellowstone recently found that larger wolves—usually three- to four-year-old males—are the most efficient hunters. Younger, lighter wolves do more chasing than killing. A wolf hunt is all about opportunity, not like in soccer, baseball, or football where each player has a specific position to maintain. Any member of the pack close enough to grab the prey, will. Another benefit of hunting in a group? Less of the kill is lost to predators, like ravens, with more wolves around.

PACK TERRITORY

There's an old Russian proverb that says, "A wolf is kept fed by his feet." If you think of a wolf pack's territory as a refrigerator, can you imagine having to jog 6 miles (9.7 km) there and back each time you felt like having a snack? A wolf is always searching for his next meal, on foot. He might walk eight hours a day in search of food. At the same time, he's patrolling his territory to make sure other wolves don't snack on any of his "groceries" (those delicious hooved animals scattered across the land-scape). A wolf's phenomenal ability to cover distance on foot is a very important adaptation for finding food.

TO MOVE QUICKLY THROUGH THE SNOW, WOLVES FOLLOW THEIR LEADER, STEPPING IN THE SAME PAWPRINTS MADE BY THEIR HUGE, BLOCKY PAWS.

In Yellowstone National Park a pack of wild gray wolves isolates a bison cow in a fresh layer of snow on a frozen creek.

AWESOME ADAPTATIONS

Prey may sometimes flee into water to escape a wolf—but wolves are good swimmers and may go after them in deep water. Some wolves will even swim out into lakes to try to catch birds!

Brr! Arctic wolves live in some of the coldest places on Earth. To survive, they've developed two layers of fur to keep them warm in temperatures as low as minus 70°F (–56°C).

On the banks of the Teklanika River in Alaska's Denali National Park, a gray wolf tracks a bull moose wounded earlier by the pack.

In the Sawtooth Mountains of Idaho, U.S.A., a male gray wolf searches out a woodpecker in an aspen tree.

SNIFFING OUT SUPPER

Another adaptation that helps him find food is an impressive sense of smell. Take a look around you—what do you know about where you're sitting right now? Most of what you know about your environment comes from information provided by your eyes. It's different for a wolf. Like your family dog, much of what a wolf knows about his surroundings comes from what he can smell.

Smell helps in hunting because, even after a wolf has found a herd of elk, moose, or deer, he can't kill any old ungulate. He has to find the very young, the very old, or a sick or injured animal. A wolf's nose helps him search out the right animal to target. He might sniff the hint of an old moose whose mouth is full of tooth decay, for instance. He can smell it long before he can see it.

Once a wolf has targeted his prey, he moves upwind and stays hidden. It's like a game of hide-and-seek. But as soon as an elk detects the presence of a predator, it goes into defense mode. Its head goes up and its neck becomes rigid. Ears swivel—which way is the predator coming from? Its nose glistens and twitches. Which way to bolt? The wolf waits. He needs the prey to run before he can attack. It's much safer to attack from behind—kicks don't injure as badly as jabbing horns. Getting the prey to run also makes it easier to pick out the weak or injured.

It's bad news for the wolf if the prey stands its ground—the animal is probably in his prime and ready to fight for his life. That's not likely to be a tangle the wolf wants to engage in. But if the prey does flee, the chase is on. The first few moments are critical. If too much time elapses, the prey is likely to get away.

If the hunt fails, often the wolves will regroup and have a group hug, of sorts. They'll wrestle, play, and jump on each other like a bunch of football players cheering and giving each other high fives. Dr. Dan MacNulty believes this behavior has to do with reassuring each other that they'll kill again, or that they are safe for the moment, despite their precarious existence. It could also be to blow off steam and relieve stress.

When a hunt is successful, there's no celebrating—only eating. What do they dig into first? The viscera, or internal organs, because they are the most nutritious. First they eat the liver, heart, and intestines. Next they'll eat the flesh, bones, and hide of the animal. When they've had their fill, the rest of the pack jumps in. They wolf down whatever they can reach, sometimes pulling the carcass in all directions at once.

HUMANS VS. WOLVES

Some scientists say there is no documented account of a healthy wolf ever attacking a human. But wolves do kill cattle and sheep, leading to conflict with humans. If a wolf is preying on something he naturally would eat, like an elk or a bison, it's referred to as predation. But if he's preying on livestock, it's called depredation and that act could put a wolf's life at risk. Although wolves generally prefer their own wild prey (they've been known to walk through a herd of cows to get to a pronghorn), from his point of view, eating a

>> ANIMAL RESCUE!

THE VALUE OF A LIFE

Peering out the window of a small airplane on a cold winter day, Dr. John Vucetich sees wolf tracks in the snow below. The pilot banks the plane to follow the trail. Dr. Vucetich hopes they'll find a recent moose kill.

His mission? To study wolves on Isle Royale National Park, a remote wilderness island in Lake Superior, and how they impact prey populations. The project has studied the predator-prey relationship between wolves and moose for the past 50 years.

Dr. Vucetich and his wife, Leah, spend five months a year on the remote island. Leah also helps save wolves. She leads the project's intern program and conducts field and lab work. Once while observing a moose, the 800-pound (363 kg) animal ran and "hid" behind Leah as a wolf passed through the trees nearby. The Vucetiches live and work in a warm yurt, a sturdy round tent made of synthetic leather.

A scientist who has devoted his life to educating others and helping them relate to nature, Dr. Vucetich uses what he learns on the island to help people understand and empathize with wolves. He's done it for 20 years. His hope is that information and understanding will convince people to treat wolves more carefully. Because wolves and humans sometimes conflict with each other, Vucetich wants to help hunters, state wildlife managers, and citizens coexist with wolves by understanding the value of any life—whether it's the life of a human, a moose, or a wolf.

cow or a sheep is an easy meal. For the ranchers losing livestock, it's the same as stolen property.

Remember Rio from page 36? He got in trouble with depredation. In 1998, the California Wolf Center in southern California bred and released 13 endangered Mexican gray wolves into a wild, high forest on public land in eastern Arizona and western New Mexico. Rio was one of those wolves. Not long after his release, Rio fathered the first wild-born Mexican wolf pup in the United States in at least 50 years.

But cattle graze in areas where Rio and other Mexican gray wolves claimed their territories. At one point Rio and his mate began scavenging on cattle

During the Lewis and Clark expedition in 1804, William Clark wrote in his journal that he observed wolves feeding on buffalo that were "killed by accident or those too ... fat to keep up." This gray wolf gives chase to a herd of bison in Yellowstone National Park.

Wolf parents, like this male gray wolf, often let their pups eat first.

carcasses strewn on the landscape. He soon began killing livestock. To protect him and the valuable genetics that have helped save Mexican gray wolves from extinction, Rio was brought back into captivity.

His story illustrates some of the difficulties arising from wolves and humans sharing land. In his case, wildlife management enabled Rio to breed in the wild. He lived to be 15 years old in captivity, a very old age for a wolf.

>> EXPERT TIPS

Dr. Vucetich's tips to learn about wolves:

1 Think of a creature that you see on a regular basis, perhaps a wolf or a sparrow. Learn a bit about how they live—how they find food and shelter, or raise their young, or survive the winter or summer.

2 Next, imagine what it must be like to have that life. To imagine this way is called empathy. Remember that what makes you happy is not always what makes another happy. If you imagine well enough, you'll experience a number of emotions—like joy, sadness, and admiration.

3 Every day, make a choice to empathize with others from the human and nonhuman worlds. The emotions that spring from empathy will fuel your actions in caring about wolves and other creatures.

>>RESCUE ACTIVITIES

NOVICE

EAT LIKE A WOLF

Meals are an important time for wolves. They fill bellies, are an opportunity to bond, and reconfirm relationships and pecking orders. It is just the same for us humans. Food brings us together and creates a chance for us to share, talk, and form friendships. This challenge is to make, share, and eat a wolf-like meal. Use your meal as an opportunity to tell your friends and family about a wolf conservation success story.

RUN LIKE A WOLF! Wolves can go a very long time before finding a potential meal. To start this challenge, build up your appetite. Translation: Get active!

SOMETIMES IT TAKES TREKKING MANY MILES if you're a wolf looking for dinner. Head out on an easy hike, or up the ante with a longer hike that lasts most of the afternoon.

WOLVES WILL STOP FOR A DRINK if they're thirsty enough (they get most of their water from the meat they eat). Take a sip if you're getting thirsty.

EXTREME

YOUR BODY IS NOT ADAPTED FOR EATING RAW MEAT like a wolf, so you will need to cook your food first. Research some recipes and get some help to prepare a menu for you and some friends.

CHECK OUT THIS RECIPE FOR A LIVER AND HEART KEBAB. Many stores sell various kinds of liver and heart. To a wolf, these are the best parts! Preparation: Cut the liver and heart into about 1-inch (2.5 cm) cubes. Season with spices, like cumin, salt, and paprika for a Moroccan flavor. Cook on the grill until desired temperature.

VEGETARIAN ALTERNATIVE: grilled pumpkin slices. Preparation: Cut your pumpkin into slices leaving the skin on. Lightly season with olive oil and sea salt. Add ancho chili powder for a more savory flavor. Grill for about two minutes on each side until tender. Remove from grill and cut off rind before enjoying!

ADVANCED

When doing this challenge, remember your manners—or not! Wolves have rules about food. Here are some tips to make your meal more authentic:

1 Research some recipes and grab a parent to help prepare. Remember to let any adult wolves with children eat first. They can eat all of the liver, heart, and intestines if they want to.

2 Use a knife and fork if you want to, otherwise get messy and just wolf it down.

3 Got any marshmallows, gummy sweets, or ice cream? These often contain an ingredient called gelatin. Gelatin is made from skin, horns, hooves, and bones. Now that's a real wolf dessert!

HEAD TO THE STORE ON A HUNT. Start by locating your prey at the local grocery store or farmers market. Use your senses. Can you navigate to the bakery or produce section by smell alone?

STALKING SILENTLY AND QUIETLY is as important for a wolf as it is for you. In the store, hide yourself as best you can and move quickly and quietly toward your "prey" without making it flee. Once seen, a wolf's prey will either stand its ground, run, or even come toward it.

PURSUE YOUR PREY, running as fast as you can (carefully and strategically making sure no one's in the way!). Run after your prey for as much as a mile (1.6 km) in an attempt to bring it down. If you succeed, make your "kill" by biting your prey (gently, you do not want to break your teeth!).

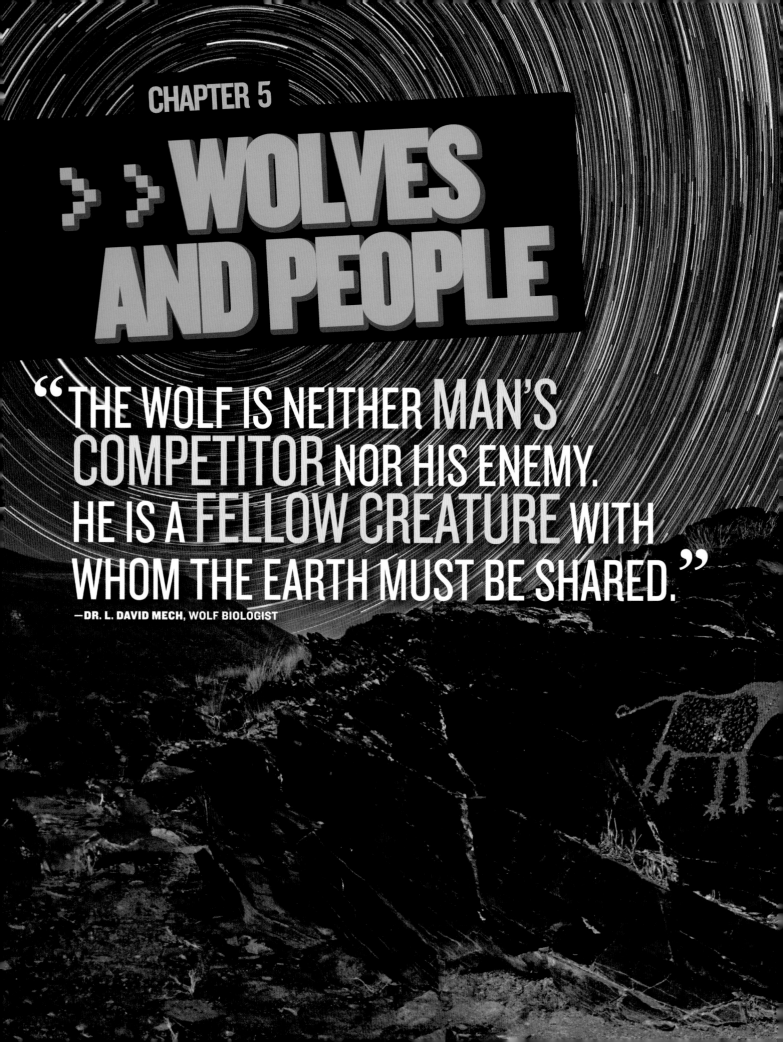

CHAPTER 5

>> WOLVES AND PEOPLE

"THE WOLF IS NEITHER MAN'S COMPETITOR NOR HIS ENEMY. HE IS A FELLOW CREATURE WITH WHOM THE EARTH MUST BE SHARED."

—DR. L. DAVID MECH, WOLF BIOLOGIST

In the Teimareh Valley in the
Zagros Mountains of Iran, star
trails and ancient petroglyphs (or
rock engravings) depicting wolves
date back 4,500 to 17,000 years.

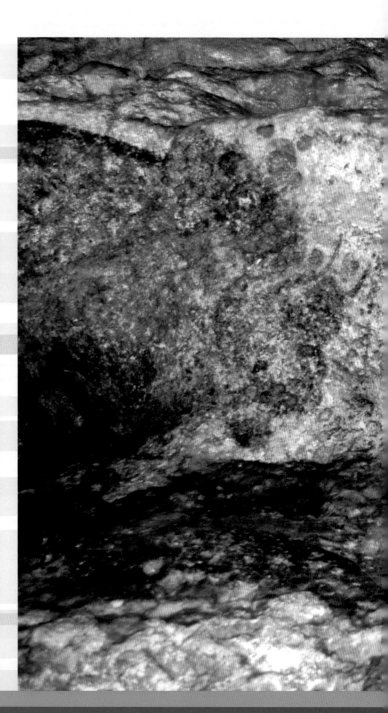

Wolves and humans have a long and complicated history, with confusion between fact and fiction. Flip open your history book from school and you're likely to find stories of ancient cultures that lived in harmony with wildlife. Historians and scientists think early humans had positive relationships with wolves. Many civilizations respected, observed, and learned from their wild neighbors.

>> **ANIMAL RESCUE!**

HELPING ITALY'S WOLVES

Biologists like Luigi Boitani at the University of Rome in Italy have helped to change people's perceptions of wolves in Europe. In 1972, when the conservation program undertaken by the University of Rome first started, wolves were unprotected and hunted.

Boitani's program launched a huge television, radio, and newspaper campaign and eventually succeeded in convincing the government that wolves were disappearing from most of their natural range in central and southern Italy. He helped change laws to give wolves full protection and outlaw the use of poison baits. In a few years, the wolf population grew to repopulate much of its former range in Italy.

Boitani believed that children were often afraid of wolves because of the legends and stories they had heard. As part of the university's program, he made a huge, personal effort to replace fiction with fact. He has given hundreds of presentations to schools across Italy, sharing facts about wolves. Today, the general knowledge about wolves in Italy has improved tremendously, thanks in part to the University of Rome's wolf conservation program.

WOLVES WORSHIPPED

Could a wolf hurt a human? Absolutely. These animals have the ability to crack open the skull of a moose with a few bites. But shy wolves rarely attack people. In fact, even if you spend time around wolves, you're more likely to be killed by a strike of lightning or a bee sting than be killed or even attacked by a wolf.

Even the mother of the world's most well-known wolf photographer didn't understand that wolves are much more afraid of people than we are afraid of them. Deep into wildlife photographer Jim Brandenburg's 40-year career documenting the lives of wolves, his Norwegian-born mother held on to old-world perceptions and fears about the animals. She worried he'd be attacked by a wolf. "Be careful that the wolves don't get you," she would warn.

Some of the earliest humans worshipped wolves, immortalizing them in paintings and engravings on the walls of underground caves that still exist today. In central France, Font de Gaume Cave is a natural museum showcasing Ice Age engravings and paintings from around 14,000 B.C.—when the world teemed with wildlife and Neanderthals used flint blades to create art on cave walls.

Deep inside Font de Gaume Cave you'll find hundreds of engravings and multicolored paintings of animals including mammoths, lions, horses, reindeer, a wolf, a bear, and rhinoceroses.

Font de Gaume Cave in France is the home to more than 200 ancient paintings, including bison (pictured), horses, mammoths, a wolf, and more.

Bob Danielson, a member of the Ojibwa tribe, wears a wolf pelt at a powwow in northern Minnesota.

OOKAMI, THE JAPANESE WORD FOR WOLF, MEANS GREAT GOD.

Some scientists believe man's tolerance and high regard for wolves led to the domestication of wolves 15,000 to 20,000 years ago. It may have started when wolves scavenged food scraps around human communities. These early humans may have appreciated the wolves' removal of trash and protection from other predators (like bears, wild boars, or lions, depending where they lived). In this case, wolves were not only tolerated, they were welcomed. On the other hand, some scientists believe that domestic dogs evolved separately from wolves about 150,000 years ago. It's another one of those great scientific debates.

HONORING THE WOLF

Civilizations throughout history worshipped wolves. Ancient Japanese shoguns built mountain shrines to honor the beloved wolf. Vikings used images of wolves as their totems, or emblems, as a symbol of strength and power. And some historians credit wolves with saving the founders of Rome. According to myth, a female wolf nursed twin baby brothers (Romulus and Remus, sons of the god Mars and a human priestess) who had been abandoned near the Tiber River. The real-life cave in Rome where archaeologists believe the babies were nurtured by the wolf is called Lupercale. The name comes from the Latin word for wolf, *lupus*. The babies survived and are thought to have later founded the city.

Native Americans revered the wolf as healing "medicine animals." The Inuit people of North America believed that a lone wolf named Amarok took care of caribou herds, preying on the weak and the sick, maintaining the herds so tribes could hunt healthy animals. Native American songs and legends portray wolves as spiritual leaders with powerful magic. Some tribes believed that wolves were once people and could be called upon for help, like guardian angels. Others wore wolf pelts while hunting to bring them power and luck. Native Americans in Yellowstone may have even bred their hunting dogs with wolves in order to maintain the fitness and prowess of their dogs.

The Nunamiuts in Alaska observed and learned from wolves' hunting skills. They revered wolves but— like many other Inuit (people native to the Arctic)— also hunted wolves. The wolves were sometimes honored with rituals of gratitude. Their pelts provided an important raw material for trading.

Gradually, civilizations around the world evolved from communal (or shared) relationships with the Earth and its living creatures to more agricultural lifestyles, setting up permanent homes and farms. As people in Europe and Asia began to claim territory for livestock, they needed a lot more space and natural resources for grazing their animals. Axes cut down forests; deadly poison cleared wolves from the landscape.

FEAR AND FAIRY TALES

Livestock equals money. In the earliest agricultural societies, if a wolf killed a cow, a sheep, or a chicken, he was no longer a respected neighbor, he was a thief. It didn't matter that humans had killed much of wolves' natural prey (the ungulates, like deer and elk, that both humans and wolves eat) or that humans had replaced wolves' habitat with farms.

The wolf's reputation underwent a transformation from angelic healer and a symbol of power to a hated thief. In the Middle Ages, wolves were exterminated in an organized fashion for the first time. During this time, dogs were bred for hunting wolves, like the borzoi, a Russian breed used in large groups. The Romans bred dogs—similar to Irish wolfhounds of today—specifically for hunting wolves.

Many religions used the thieving wolf as a demonic symbol, a physical incarnation of evil. Superstitions about wolves swirled and became known as fact. Bloodthirsty villains, wolves played starring roles in European legends and fairy tales.

In Japan, where people once prayed to wolves, people in the late 1800s began poisoning wolves to make room for modern agriculture. A wild wolf hasn't been seen in Japan since 1905.

Humans in Europe and Asia began shooting, trapping, and poisoning wolves. When they sought a new world, which would become America, their ideas came with them. Settlers in the New World did what they had done in the Old World: clear entire regions of trees and predators to make spacious, safe grazing areas for livestock.

LEARNING ABOUT WOLVES

Why did people become so afraid of wolves? Likely it was because they didn't know much about the mysterious species. By the early 1900s in the United States, *(continued on p. 89)*

>> MEET A WOLF

THE BIG BAD WOLF

Are you afraid of the big, bad wolf? A lot of people are. For centuries, European fairy tales have shaped the way generations of people imagine the nightmarish "big bad wolf." In Russian composer Sergei Prokofiev's original story "Peter and the Wolf" (played out in a symphony), the wolf is a terrifying creature given life through the ominous sounds of the French horn.

The unforgivable wolf in the French story "Little Red Riding Hood" stalks a little girl on the way to see her sick grandmother, eats the grandmother, then tries to trick the girl so he can eat her, too.

In the "Three Little Pigs," a story that originated in England, three youngsters leave home and venture out into the world. A relentless "big bad wolf" torments them and threatens to blow each of their houses down and eat the pigs. Modern versions of these stories in books, cartoons, and movies characterize wolves as sinister killers with glowing yellow eyes and gigantic teeth dripping with blood.

Now that you know what you know about shy, family-oriented wolves, can you distinguish fact from fiction?

ENGLAND'S LAST WOLF WAS KILLED IN THE EARLY 16TH CENTURY UNDER KING HENRY VIII.

LUIGI BOITANI

BORN: ROME, ITALY
JOB TITLE: PROFESSOR OF CONSERVATION, BIOLOGY
AFFILIATION: UNIVERSITY OF ROME, ITALY
JOB LOCATION: ROME, ITALY
YEARS WORKING WITH WOLVES: 40
MONTHS A YEAR IN THE FIELD: 2–3

How are you helping to save wolves?

I help wolf conservation through an integrated program of scientific research, assistance to policy makers and politicians dealing with wolf-human conflicts, and public education. Wolf conservation requires us to find solutions for humans to coexist with nature, even when nature has some negative impact on our lives.

Favorite thing about your job?

I love being with wolves, following their tracks in the snow, howling to them in the night, and watching them. I never tire of being in the field trying to capture some new information about wolf biology. It's exciting and every day I learn something new.

Best thing about working in the field?

Being close to nature is my purpose in life. I am curious and interested in anything that happens in the wild. Nature never misleads. Instead, it provides exciting opportunities to satisfy my curiosity. Wolves are so adaptable to a huge variety of situations and behave so differently in various contexts that I never get tired of studying them.

Worst thing about working in the field?

Nature can be tough. Sometimes it challenges my resistance. But if you take these challenges as a test for how much you want to live in harmony with nature, you'll pass the test. Wolves are often nocturnal animals. Being out in the woods alone at night, in the winter, means cold hands and snow. But humans—politicians, policy makers, angry farmers, and aggressive hunters—can be far worse than any natural challenge.

How can kids prepare to do your job one day?

Get a university degree in biology, ecology, and behavior. Then apply to be a volunteer at a good wolf research project in the field. Learn from an experienced researcher about the complexities of wolf conservation. Most important, cultivate your curiosity; feed it with new ideas and projects.

In February 2004, wolf MI5 was found injured by a car on the highway in northern Italy. A local veterinarian examined the animal and thought it might survive. I suggested he fit it with a satellite collar so we could follow his movements after release. MI5 eventually traveled more than 600 miles (1,000 km), across mountains, highways, rivers, and railways. He ended up in France. This wolf provided the first solid evidence that recolonization of distant areas is well within the biological possibility of wolves, even in the human-dominated landscapes of central and southern Europe. MI5 had a huge positive impact on the public opinion of wolves in France and Italy.

Two wolves pad through the snow in Bavarian Forest National Park in Germany.

Filmmaker Bob Landis's
tips to learn about wolves:

1

Read as much as pos-
sible about wolves—
books, articles,
and magazines.

2

Learn and
follow the
politics of
wolves around
the world.

3

Immerse yourself in
groups of people who
share your love of
learning about wolves.

The human and wolf worlds collide as
a black wolf follows a winding road
through Yellowstone National Park.

wolves had been almost entirely eliminated to protect livestock. At that time, wolves' prey species had been wiped out to make room for sheep and cows.

In the 1940s, things changed in the U.S. when scientists began to wonder if eradicating "pests" like wolves was doing more harm than good. An era of conservation began. People began to think more about our environment and the other animals in it. Over the next few decades, many scientists studied wolves and debated their role in the environment. This led to government protections and reintroduction programs. Tolerance for wolves and other wild creatures grew. Today, prey populations for wolves, like elk, have rebounded to support wolf populations. Factors like harsh winter weather and disease kill much more livestock than wolves do.

But let's face it: Modern humans don't have a good track record when it comes to putting wildlife first. Skyscrapers, shopping malls, and housing developments crowd open spaces. Highways cut through forests. Builders fill wetlands to make room for more homes. Our planet's rain forests are being leveled at an alarming rate.

In Europe, on the island of Britain (home to England, Scotland, and Wales) all top carnivores—including the wolves who roamed the earth from north to south, and east to west, for hundreds of thousands of years before—have been killed off by humans. As a result, the deer population has exploded, destroying the vegetation that feeds and shelters other wildlife and devastating the fragile island ecosystem.

CLIMATE CHANGE

The threat of man-made climate change may be one of the most important challenges we humans face today.

Loss of top predators changes the food chain right down to microorganisms in the soil, just like the disappearance of sharks in the world's oceans negatively impacts sea creatures from seals and fish, all the way down to microscopic plankton. Maybe it's because predators like wolves, lions, tigers, bears, and sharks don't get along well with people. But maybe it's the other way around. Maybe people need to do a better job of getting along with our world's top predators.

That's not all. Some scientists believe that humans' destruction of our planet can, or already has started to, cause a serious climate shift that could start a domino effect of habitat destruction and extinction for many species. Five mass extinctions have occurred in Earth's history, caused by natural phenomena, like massive volcanic eruptions or meteor strikes from outer space. Are we in the midst of the sixth, this time

ANIMAL SUPERPOWERS — WOLVES AND HUMANS ARE A LOT ALIKE

WOLVES LIKE TO HANG OUT WITH THEIR FAMILIES, GO FOR LONG WALKS, AND EAT AT THE SAME "TABLE."

WOLVES DON'T USE FENCES, BUT—LIKE HUMANS—THEY ARE VERY TERRITORIAL.

WOLVES INVESTIGATE BY SPYING, LISTENING, AND SNIFFING, JUST AS PEOPLE DO!

In Kalispell, Montana, U.S.A., hunters protest how the federal government has managed wolf populations.

caused by human destruction? Can we reverse its effects by taking better care of our planet?

HUNTING WOLVES

Despite the comeback of many wolf populations these days, many of the same old challenges threaten wolves. These peaceful, family-oriented animals continue to suffer habitat loss as human populations continue to claim wildlife areas. Many hunters still love the thrill of a wolf hunt and bringing home an impressive game trophy.

Now that wolves in the northern Rockies of the U.S. have reached healthy numbers and are no longer listed as an endangered species, wolves outside of Yellowstone National Park are managed by individual states' natural resources agencies. Because they are no longer endangered, wolves in this region have joined the ranks of the many mammals that can be hunted for recreation. In general, the rules that states use to regulate wolf hunting are the same they use for hunting black bear, moose, elk, and deer. In states like Montana, Idaho, or Wyoming, where hunting is a tradition, anyone can apply for a permit to hunt a wolf. One exception is most of Wyoming, beyond the northwestern corner of the state, where people can kill wolves any time by any means.

Cattle ranchers don't kill wolves themselves, but state wildlife management officials will do the deed, lawfully—often by helicopter or small plane—if a wolf is known to be killing livestock.

No matter who's hunting wolves for what reason, it's a controversial subject. Conflict is a constant in the

THE HERD'S REAL DANGER

In the United States, wolves are not the number one killer of domestic cattle and calves. Check out the list to see what is munching on ranchers' cows:

#1 Coyotes are the number one predator of livestock. They also are known to chomp on farmers' irrigation pipes.

#2 Wild cats, like mountain lions, lynx, and bobcats, will sometimes cover their kill with debris from the area and come back for it later.

#3 Black vultures will often attack calves, who are easy prey for these birds.

#4 Domestic dogs are a problem, especially in areas where livestock are close to cities and suburbs.

#5 Wolves are number five on the list. Surprised?

An arctic wolf gets curious about a human camp on Ellesmere Island in the Canadian Arctic.

WOLVES IN BULGARIA

Bulgarian wolf biologist Elena Tsingarska cradles a wild wolf's head in her hands as she straps a radio transmitting collar around his neck. Her hands touch his coarse fur and she looks into his eyes. Words can't quite explain the feeling of the moment.

Tsingarska has studied wolves in Bulgaria for almost 20 years, braving often cold and wet conditions to spend seven or eight months a year in the field. She collects data about different aspects of the wolf population as the leader of the Balkani Wildlife Society in Bulgaria. She created a wolf management plan to maintain a wolf population there.

When she's not in the field, Tsingarska shares what she's learned through educational programs in schools. Ten years ago, she helped establish the Large Carnivore Education Centre, based in a Bulgarian village called Vlahi in the foothills of the Pirin Mountains. The center is home to ambassador wolves and bears. It has educated thousands of children and adults about the importance of saving wolves, bears, and other wild animals in eastern Europe.

story of wolves and humans. We are both large carnivores, competing for space and food. The hunting of wolves revolves around this conflict.

GETTING TOO CLOSE

You've probably heard someone say about an animal or an insect: "It's more afraid of you, than you are of it." The same is mostly true about wolves. Rare exceptions come when a wolf is sick with rabies or has gotten too used to having humans around, like bears that raid campsites for food or garbage, or baboons in Africa who demand to be fed by tourists. In these cases, the wild animals have been rewarded for tangling with humans. The same thing can happen with wolves.

When a wild animal comes in close contact with humans, it becomes a life-threatening moment for everyone involved. The human could be injured and the wolf could be killed for doing what comes naturally to him. We should certainly not approach wolves with the fear that many of our ancestors did, but they deserve respect and distance—the same as any wild animal.

The few human-wolf encounters that have led to injuries are usually cases of mistaken identity, similar to shark attacks where from below the surface of the water, a shark mistakes a human on a surfboard for a seal. Wolves generally are afraid of humans, perhaps because they have been persecuted by humans for so much of their history. It's rare enough to spot a wolf in the wild, let alone have an encounter that would lead to an injury. And for an animal who can easily kill a 2,000-pound (907 kg) bison, they certainly have the capability to kill humans—but they don't seem to want to.

People have been taught to think of wolves as scary predators. But like with sharks, humans kill a lot more wolves than wolves kill humans. Like most wild animals, wolves just want to be left alone. They deserve their place on Earth like any other living creature. If we don't bother them, they won't bother us.

Every human has the power to positively impact wolves. What impact will you make?

>>RESCUE ACTIVITIES

USE YOUR POWER

You have the power to change the world. By sharing your thoughts, ideas, and opinions you can change things for the better. You may know a wolf or have never seen a wolf before. Either way, you can help to protect the habitats that wolves live in and save wolves.

In this challenge you will choose, write, share, and send words that will shift public opinion of wolves and improve their reputation. By writing and sharing these words you will be contributing to an international effort to save wolves.

NOVICE

RESEARCH A POWERFUL PETITION. A petition is a statement or request that lots of people sign to show that they agree with it.

RESEARCH GROUPS PETITIONING FOR CHANGE. Start online and write to them to come petition in your area. Volunteer with the group to help out.

SIGN THE PETITION. Throw your name to the wolves!

EXTREME

CREATE A PETITION. When tens, hundreds, or even thousands of people sign a petition it can be a powerful way to demonstrate support for a point of view. By making a petition on behalf of wolves you can help to protect them.

RESEARCH A PARTICULAR WOLF, PACK OF WOLVES, OR HABITAT THAT IS IN TROUBLE. Take some time to do lots of research and make sure you know all about it. Collecting evidence to support your argument will help you to gain support and influence.

START SUPPORT FOR YOUR PETITION ONLINE. Get it out there in as many ways as possible. Create posters and establish tables at local stores with their permission.

Wolf expert Jim Dutcher bottle-feeds a wolf pup.

Create a powerful message by persuading the reader to agree with your opinion. Describing the problem, explaining it using evidence, including facts, and proposing solutions are the four main steps to take when crafting your message.

1

Send it to the media. Share a copy of the letter and list of supporters with local or national bloggers, radio stations, and newspapers. Try to get your message or petition out to well-known people, public officials, and politicians.

2

Be social by gathering signatures of support and sharing your final petition online. Using a website to create an online ePetition will help you to do this. Ask everyone that signs to tweet, share, and "like" the petition.

3

Be visual. Pictures, videos, and maps can all be powerful ways to communicate stories, issues, and problems. If you can, make your letter visual and include pictures of wolves. This will help your supporters to connect to the issue.

ADVANCED

WHO HAS THE POWER TO HELP THE WOLVES? Perhaps there is a government that does not want wolves to be reintroduced into the wild or a hunting organization that wants to remove wolves from an area. Find out who is in charge. These are the people you are going to write to.

WRITE A LETTER TO THE POWERFUL PERSON THAT YOU HAVE IDENTIFIED. Take your time to present your argument. Give evidence and examples for each point that you make. This is your chance to help wolves by representing them.

ONCE YOUR LETTER IS FINISHED IT IS TIME TO GET AS MANY PEOPLE AS YOU CAN TO SIGN IT. The more people that sign it, the more powerful your words will become. As well as getting physical signatures you could also run your petition online.

Once you have gathered together as many supporters as you can, send your petition to the people who have the power to save wolves. With some skill and a bit of luck, your efforts may just help to protect wolves now or in the future.

A gray wolf howls to his pack at sunset.

CHAPTER 6

> > SAVING WOLVES

" THE ABILITY OF WOLVES TO EXPERIENCE COMPASSION AND EMPATHY IS THE SINGLE MOST IMPORTANT MESSAGE ABOUT WOLVES WE CAN SHARE. "

—JIM AND JAMIE DUTCHER, CO-FOUNDERS OF LIVING WITH WOLVES

Pgnant with her first litter of pups in the spring of 1996, Yellowstone wolf #7 settled into a den in the cool ground under a huge Douglas fir tree. She and her mate, a large black wolf known as #2, had found each other after leaving their natal (birth) packs. Both of their packs—the Crystal Creek Pack and the Rose Creek Pack—had been moved to Yellowstone National Park from Alberta, Canada, to hopefully form a wild pack.

WILL THEY SURVIVE?

Young adults, #7 and #2 paired up and established territory on the Blacktail Plateau in northern Yellowstone, a high grassland surrounded by evergreen trees. If they survived, they would lead the first naturally-formed wild pack in the park since 1929.

Dr. Dan MacNulty sat on a windy hilltop watching the wolves through a spotting scope. Part of the team of scientists helping with the reintroduction of wolves into Yellowstone, Dr. MacNulty's job was studying how wolves hunted and their impact on the elk population.

The pregnant wolf lay in the den waiting for her pups to be born. Dr. MacNulty wondered if the male would be able to secure enough food to save the pair of wolves and their unborn pups. Hunting alone presented a challenge even for experienced wolves. Day after day, #2 set off to hunt. Day after day, he returned without a kill.

But #2 was an exceptional hunter. One day, he returned carrying meat from an elk kill. Scarfing her food, #7 couldn't have known that her mate was also helping to save generations of wolves to come in the northern Rockies. And she couldn't have known about all the people working to give these wolves a chance to start a new pack.

Not long after that day, #7 gave birth to a healthy litter. She protected the pups against other wolves and predators. The pack thrived. It was later named the Leopold Pack after Aldo Leopold, the man who many consider to be the founder of wildlife conservation in the United States and one of the first people to suggest wolf reintroduction to Yellowstone.

ATKA

Atka the arctic wolf lives a more pampered life than his wild cousins—caretakers serve his food every day and he never has to fight for his territory. As an ambassador wolf at the Wolf Conservation Center in South Salem, New York, U.S.A., Atka helps educate the public about wolves just by being himself—either on exhibit at the center or traveling in an air-conditioned van. His favorite road-trip snack? Double cheeseburgers, hold the pickles!

An environmental education organization, the Wolf Conservation Center teaches people about wolves and how to protect their future. In a single year Atka might visit more than 150 schools, nature centers, museums (once even on an aircraft carrier), and libraries to spread the word, or should we say, howl it out?

Atka has even helped teach lawmakers in our nation's capital about wolves. Atka puts a beautiful, furry face on the cause, helping legislators and the public understand what's involved with recovering an endangered species. During one Washington, D.C., trip, Atka even left a distinct "mark" on the floor of a banquet room in a U.S. House of Representatives office building.

WOLVES MAY SLEEP FOR 12 TO 16 HOURS AFTER A HUNT, BUT CAN TAKE OFF AT A MOMENT'S NOTICE.

As an ambassador wolf, Atka provides a living connection between people and wild wolves.

Kira Cassidy, a biological field technician with the Yellowstone Wolf Project, takes a telemetry reading near a group of wolf watchers in Yellowstone National Park's Lamar Valley, Wyoming, U.S.A. Telemetry is used to track and listen to wolves through radio collars.

GENETIC TESTING SHOWS THAT GRAY FEMALE WOLVES REPRODUCE MORE SUCCESSFULLY THAN BLACK-COATED FEMALE WOLVES, BUT BLACK-COATED FEMALES TEND TO LIVE LONGER.

As leaders of the Leopold Pack, #2 and #7 had a new litter of pups every year for the next seven years. You know one of their pups—the furry jet-black pup that grew up to be the charming and unpredictable Yellowstone wolf #302. Other descendants of this successful breeding pair still roam the Blacktail Plateau today, thanks to wolf biologists like Dr. MacNulty working to save wolves, and thanks to the perseverance and relentless spirit of wolves like #7 and #2.

OUTDOOR LABORATORY

Reintroducing wolves into Yellowstone National Park after a 70-year absence has given scientists the opportunity to study these top predators in what Dr. MacNulty calls "the perfect outdoor laboratory." Since the reintroduction, wolf populations have thrived, helping restore the natural process of predation to the park.

Yellowstone is a protected, large-scale wild system unlike any other. It's a wilderness landscape where wolf populations can behave according to their own instincts and where scientists can study the relationships between predator and prey as well as wolves' relationships with other animals in the ecosystem.

In Arizona and New Mexico, the U.S. Fish and Wildlife Service reintroduced captive-bred Mexican gray wolves into public lands in the Apache National Forest. Before this recovery program, wolves had been gone for 30 years. In 2013, 46 Mexican gray wolves kept scientists and biologists busy with data from their radio collars, sharing information about where they go and what they do.

RED WOLF FOSTER PROGRAM

Her belly full of milk and eyes still shut at nine days old, the furry red wolf pup (actually more brown than red) snuggled into the hand of the field specialist caring for her. The only survivor of a captive litter born in late April 2013 at the Sandy Ridge Captive Red Wolf Facility in North Carolina, the little female was on her way to the *wild* life in the swampy Alligator River National Wildlife Refuge.

When the timing works out for this delicate adoptive process, the U.S. Fish and Wildlife Service's Red Wolf Recovery Program places captive pups into wild litters. This helps increase the numbers of wild red wolves and enhances the genetic diversity of the wild population. In order for it to work out, the captive litter must be born close to the time the wild litter is born. The wild litter has to be small enough to support an addition. And it works best if the foster pups are less than two weeks old, to take advantage of Mom's strong maternal instincts.

On that spring day in North Carolina, the field specialist doused the red wolf pup with urine from the two other pups in the litter (so the parents would accept her) and put her in the puppy pile. When all three pups grow big enough, they'll be trapped and fitted with radio collars so biologists can study their movement and behavior to further help the recovery of the red wolf, one of the world's most endangered canids.

SEEING WOLVES IN THE WILD

Unless you live in wolf country, you probably don't see wild wolves often. But that doesn't mean you can't help save wolves.

In Scotland, people burned dense forests to eliminate the last wolves 200 years ago. But today, government agencies, scientists, and conservation groups are collaborating on programs to reintroduce wolves. More than 50 wolf conservation groups around the world work to save wolves—creating documentaries, educating the public, and raising money.

The reappearance of wolves in wild areas has given ecotourism in Europe a boost. In Spain, visitors from all over the world fill hotels and restaurants near La Culebra mountain range, hoping to see wild wolves. In 2011, a wolf was spotted in the Veluwe National Park in

>> ANIMAL RESCUE!

LIVING WITH WOLVES >> > >

From the time they first bottle-fed newborn wolf puppies, wildlife experts Jim and Jamie Dutcher started learning life lessons from wolves.

The Dutchers have studied wolves for more than 20 years, basing their own lives on sharing what wolves have taught them about compassion, forgiveness, and strong family ties. Observing and documenting the social lives of wolves up close, they lived among the Sawtooth Pack for six years, and were accepted by the wolves. Jim and Jamie made their home in a tented camp bordering Idaho's Sawtooth Wilderness, producing three award-winning documentaries and revealing important insights about the pack. Their book *The Hidden Life of Wolves*, published by National Geographic, is filled with beautiful photographs and information aimed to teach the world about this misunderstood animal.

The Sawtooth Pack, ambassadors for all wolves, also serves as the basis of the Dutchers' nonprofit organization, Living With Wolves. Beginning with the Dutchers' own experiences, the nonprofit has been joined by many thousands of supporters, all focused on making a difference for wolves. The organization's photographic exhibit tours museums in the United States, while Living With Wolves works to share vital information that can change hearts and minds by dispelling myth and misinformation. It also provides on-the-ground information to the public and national and local wildlife managers. Jim and Jamie meet personally with people all over America and even overseas, presenting programs and interviews, and also reach out to students in classrooms by Skype and in person.

Dedicated to raising awareness about wolves, Living With Wolves shares the fascinating observations that the Dutchers originally learned about wolves—tolerant, curious, and intelligent animals with emotional lives that are similar to those of humans—and how important wolves are to maintaining healthy ecosystems.

Like the Native Americans who respected wolves and may even have learned how to hunt by watching wolves, the Dutchers know we can all learn from these canines of the forest.

To learn more about the Dutchers and Living With Wolves, visit their website at www.livingwithwolves.org.

An inquisitive and affectionate wolf pup sniffs wolf expert Jamie Dutcher.

IN YELLOWSTONE NATIONAL PARK, HUNTING WOLVES IS NOT ALLOWED.

FOOD FIGHT <<<

Livestock carcasses left out on a ranch are like text messages sent to all the wolves in the area saying "free food!" Once a wolf arrives, he might develop a taste for live calves. Depredation on livestock can mean death for a wolf.

Dr. Seth Wilson saves wolves by helping ranchers in Montana's cattle country reduce livestock losses from wild predators. Fewer livestock kills mean less pressure for state authorities to remove or kill wolves. He works for two organizations, The Blackfoot Challenge and People and Carnivores, both of which help ranchers and wolves coexist.

On a typical day at work, Dr. Wilson might help a rancher set up electric fencing to keep wolves away from newborn calves or remove livestock carcasses. He might hike around in the mountains looking for signs of wolves. Sometimes his job involves long days in a hot, dusty field vehicle. He also holds meetings to help find common ground between ranchers who might want to see all wolves gone and conservationists who want all wolves saved.

His job also involves some welcome surprises. Once he was out looking for wolves and found 14 turtles basking on a rock in a river. Another time he discovered four great horned owls sitting next to a creek.

Over the past six years, the number of wolves in Montana's Blackfoot Valley has increased, but the number of conflicts has stayed at a low level. That's good news. In the future, Dr. Wilson hopes to help ranching communities in the states of Washington, Oregon, and northern California better coexist with wolves. His ultimate dream: to find a balance for both wolves and people in the landscape that we share.

Seth Wilson (right) works with rancher Jay Coughlin (left) on an electric fence to protect his farm's livestock.

Holland for the first time since 1898. Wolves have also returned to Sweden, France, Italy, Portugal, and most of eastern Europe.

In the U.S., tourists travel to Alaska from all over the world hoping for the chance to see a beautiful arctic wolf in the wild. Rebounding populations of wolves in Yellowstone have brought great news for lovers of wildlife. There's no better or easier place in the world to catch a glimpse of a wild wolf. Ecotourism has boomed with the return of the wolf. Local businesses have grown as tourists pour into the area to see wolves.

Today—in most places—wolves are more valuable alive than dead.

"Rewilding Europe" is an initiative by World Wildlife Fund Netherlands and other European conservation groups. Their plan? To "rewild" wolves, bison, red deer, wild horses, moose, wild boars, wild reindeer, and more on at least 2.5 million acres (1 million hectares) of Europe by 2020.

There's lots of good news, but of course there are challenges, too.

PROTECTING LIVESTOCK

More wolves means more interaction between wolves and people and the potential for livestock to be killed by wolves. Many ranchers come up with solutions for protection of valuable herds that don't involve killing wolves, like use of livestock guard dogs. Unlike the ancient dogs bred to hunt wolves, these breeds were developed to protect flocks of sheep and herds of cows from predators.

Livestock guardian dog Maggie is a 100-pound (45 kg), tawny-coated Anatolian shepherd who helps her family guard 1,500 head of sheep and cattle at Candll Ranch in northern Saskatchewan, Canada. Like her ancestors have for 6,000 years in Turkey's harsh mountainous climate, Maggie guards livestock against predators. Five-year-old Maggie is a strong

Wildlife photographer Jim Brandenburg's tips for how kids can share the story of the wolf:

1 Learn all you can. The more you know about the wolf the more passionate you'll become. Share what you learn about wolves with your friends and family to shed light on the old myths.

2 If you don't believe people should hunt wolves, write a letter to lawmakers in your state. Join the International Wolf Center, or any organization that tries to help wolves.

3 Ask your parents to take you to a park, like Yellowstone National Park, where you can see wolves in their own habitat. In the meantime, take photographs of wild animals in your own backyard, like a squirrel or a bird. Maybe one day you'll gct to photograph a wild wolf!

Livestock guardian dogs, like this Maremma sheepdog in Germany, help stop the cycle of depredation by discouraging wolves from killing cows and sheep.

protector of her herd and wears scars from her encounters with coyotes and wolves.

She doesn't work alone. While Maggie patrols the ranch—sometimes traveling 2 miles (3 km) between flocks to check up on them—Hannah, the 100-pound (45 kg) fluffy white Great Pyrenees, sticks closer to her herd. Hafiz, the fiercely protective, 150-pound (68 kg) Kangal dog, patrols miles every day along the ranch perimeter, barking to warn predators off or threatening an attack if they come near a sheep or cow.

Grizzly and Matilda are two of Maggie's six-month-old pups who are training as future sheep protectors, spending time with the herd and learning from the older dogs.

Since Maggie and her team joined the ranch, wolves and coyotes don't linger. Maggie may not know it, but she and her co-workers are saving wolves and helping ranchers and wolves to coexist.

WOLVES ARE HYPER-CARNIVORES, WHICH MEANS THEY SOMETIMES EAT THINGS OTHER THAN MEAT, LIKE GRASS OR FRUIT.

REVOLUTIONARY RANCHERS

When you leave your house, it's a good idea to shut the door behind you, right? How ranchers take care of their livestock can mean the difference between a door wide open to wolves, and one shut tight. "Husbandry" is the term for how someone takes care of their livestock.

Husbandry techniques include electric fencing to keep livestock safe. RAG (radio active guard) devices string together strobe lights, bells, and loudspeakers that set off an awful racket when a radio-collared wolf comes within range. All that noise and light is likely to send a wolf—even a hungry one—in the opposite direction.

Other ranching techniques mimic safety precautions taken by wild ungulates. Farmers bunch their cows together in temporary corrals to keep them safe, much like wild bison crowd around each other for protection in the wild. Ranchers can also time livestock pregnancies so births happen around the same time—newborn calves and

>> WOLF SPOTLIGHT

DO YOU WOLF YOUR FOOD?

Do your parents insist on good manners at the dinner table—like putting your napkin on your lap and chewing with your mouth closed? Wolves—wild or captive—are not held to the same standard. Check out how wolves eat. And don't even think about trying these table manners at home!

Mediterranean wolves scavenge garbage dumps for food.

After a kill, one wolf anchors the carcass as the other tears the skin with his teeth.

lambs are easier to keep safe that way. It's the way deer, moose, bison, and elk operate to keep their babies safe.

Another tip from the wild? Horns. Big ones. Some ranchers in the western United States mix large, horned corriente cattle in with their domestic herds. Not only do the horned cattle have more weaponry, they are aggressive if threatened. Mixing in a few horned cattle is like mixing in a "guard cow" (or an attack cow!): It's a protective role. Unlike most domestic cows, corriente cattle—descendants of the conquistadors' cattle from the 15th century—are not entirely domesticated. Their sharp horns could send a wolf flying—easy.

SAFE COWS, SAFE WOLVES

Protecting cows helps save wolves by preventing the cycle of depredation from continuing. It's a recurring theme in managing the complicated relationship between cattle ranchers and wolves. There's a 68-year-old cowboy in Montana named Jim Powers who has devoted years of his life to protecting cattle.

Powers has a set of skills vital for protecting animals. As range riders, he and his wife Marilyn (and 16 horses) camp out at a "cow camp" for months during the summer looking after more than 1,200 head of cattle grazing on thousands of acres on predator-rich public grazing land in the Gravelly Mountains of southwestern Montana. Their grandson, a 14-year-old ranch-hand named Cameron, helps too.

Riding through the cattle on quarter horses, the Powers cover about 20 miles (32 km) a day. They check the cattle, check the water, and put out salt licks.

Powers knows cattle and how to make them less vulnerable to depredation: like moving them at a quiet pace so the calves can keep up with the moms. Or tending to sick or injured cattle swiftly so predators don't come calling.

Powers looks for signs of wolves, like tracks or remains of a fresh kill. He looks for piles of old elk bones, bird feathers, and tufts of rabbit fur. Those piles often signal a wolf den. If they come across a wolf (or a grizzly bear or a mountain lion), they do everything they can to discourage him from coming near the cows, like shooting a gun in the air and yelling.

Powers's skills as a cowboy help reduce friction between cattle ranchers and wolves. It's an important part of saving wolves. You can save wolves, too.

Wolves will cache, or hide, extra food (sometimes regurgitated, or thrown up) for later.

Wolves will eat a fresh carcass—internal organs, flesh, and anything else soft—packing their stomachs until their sides distend uncomfortably.

The first day I saw the white wolves on the tundra of Canada's high Arctic. Near my home in northern Minnesota, wolves were wary of people. But the day I saw the white wolves in the Arctic, instead of running away, they came toward me, curious and with very little fear. It was an epic moment. I ended up studying the wolves there for three years.

>> EXPLORER INTERVIEW

JIM BRANDENBURG

NAME: JIM BRANDENBURG
BORN: LUVERNE, MINNESOTA, U.S.A.
JOB TITLES: WILDLIFE AUTHOR, PHOTOGRAPHER, AND FILMMAKER; FOUNDER OF THE BRANDENBURG PRAIRIE FOUNDATION
AFFILIATIONS: NATIONAL GEOGRAPHIC SOCIETY, JIM BRANDENBURG GALLERY, AND THE BRANDENBURG PRAIRIE FOUNDATION
JOB LOCATION: ELY, MINNESOTA, U.S.A.
YEARS WORKING WITH WOLVES: 43
MONTHS A YEAR IN THE FIELD: 12, EXCEPT WHEN TRAVELING

How are you helping to save wolves?
I write books and make documentaries to help people understand the real nature of wolves. I also spend a lot of time in Europe working on wolf education.

Favorite thing about your job?
Knowing that I might have made a difference by sharing the joys and sorrows of wolves through books, presentations, photographs, and documentaries.

Best thing about working in the field?
For me, it's having a connection to the miracle of nature and all of its healing qualities.

Worst thing about working in the field?
The hardest thing is becoming emotionally attached. In Minnesota, wolf hunting is legal at certain times of the year. Some wolves that I watched grow up have been killed. To me, it's no different than seeing my family or my dog get hurt. I don't understand killing wolves for sport. I was put on this earth to tell the story of wolves. Sometimes it's very painful.

How can kids prepare for your job one day?
Learn all you can. The more you know about the wolf the more passionate you'll become. Take photographs of wild animals in your own backyard, like a squirrel or a bird. Maybe one day you'll get to photograph a wild wolf!

An arctic wolf sneaks up on photographer Jim Brandenburg while he naps on Ellesmere Island, Canada.

WORKING LIKE A DOG

Many different professionals work directly and indirectly with wolves. Vets, zoologists, wildlife police, rangers, and photographers all work directly with wolves, often meeting them in the wild or in captivity. Campaigners, cartographers, lawyers, teachers, writers, and fund-raisers are just a handful of professionals who help wolf populations and habitats, but do not physically see wolves as often, if at all.

This challenge is to do the job of a professional who works with canids, the family of animals that includes wolves, foxes, and dogs. Depending on where you live in the world you may be able to do this challenge with any of the canid family, although it will probably be easiest and safest to work with domestic dogs.

To be good at any of these professions, you need to be good at asking questions. We have suggested some things you could ask when doing each job, but you should always think of your own questions, too.

NOVICE

PROFESSION 1: FILMMAKER

PLAN AND FILM A SHORT WILDLIFE FILM ABOUT A DOG. You could ask a professional filmmaker to help you, or you can teach yourself. Your film could tell the story of going for a walk, of the dog's typical day, or the relationships it has with other dogs.

When making your film, ask yourself: Who are you making your film for? Why are you making the film? Which would be the best dog to film? What do you want to include in your film? How are you going to film it?

EXTREME

PROFESSION 3: VET

IT IS SOMETIMES POSSIBLE TO WORK-SHADOW, INTERVIEW, OR VOLUNTEER WITH YOUR LOCAL VET. Depending on where in the world you live, they might work with a wide range of different canids. Use helping your local vet as an opportunity to learn as much as you can about canids.

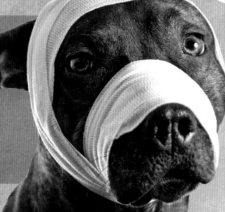

Do you want a career working with wildlife? Check out these tips to help you start out.

1 Be brave and ask. If you would like to work with your local vet, ranger, or another professional write them a warm letter, be polite, and ask. The worst that can happen is they say no ... but then they could say yes!

2 Keep a notebook of your questions, answers, and detailed notes about your experience.

3 Keep a record of your achievements. Make sure to stay in touch with your contact. You can use this evidence to support your next request to have an experience or get a job in the field.

ADVANCED

PROFESSION 2: ANIMAL PSYCHOLOGIST

IF YOU CAN, VISIT A ZOO THAT HAS A PACK OF WOLVES OR WILD DOGS.
If you cannot get to a zoo, don't worry! Take a trip to your local park and do the same job with dogs.

Use a sketchbook to keep a record of all the animals, their relationships, and what they get up to. Bring a good set of pencils and a camera to help you.

When making your observations think about these questions: Where is the best place to observe the wolves from? How can you tell the wolves apart? Can you identify which wolves have the most and least power? How many different wolf behaviors can you record? What do the different behaviors mean?

When helping the vet you could ask:
• How are canids different from other animals?
• Has he or she ever worked with wolves?
• What would be special about working with a wolf compared to other animals?
• What common problems do canids face?
• How can vets help canids?

CHAPTER 7

>>> TAKE ACTION

A wolf pack sticks together no matter where they travel! This gray wolf pack passes by a foggy pond in Idaho's Sawtooth Mountains.

"WE NEED TO ADOPT THE ATTITUDE THAT OTHER ANIMALS BESIDES HUMANS ARE IMPORTANT, TOO."

—DR. DOUG SMITH, WOLF BIOLOGIST

WOLF PUPS MIMIC THEIR ELDERS—WALKING, SNIFFING, AND LOOKING EVERYWHERE THE ADULTS DO.

If you ever encounter a wolf, be quiet and still. Always respect its space. If the wolf senses danger, often it will run away.

There aren't any wild wolves in Elizabeth Burras's Iowa, U.S.A., neighborhood, but that hasn't stopped the ten-year-old from helping to save wolves. She raises money for the International Wolf Center in Ely, Minnesota, U.S.A., by selling chocolate bars and flowers, lemonade and homemade cookies that her grandmother makes, and by selling toys and clothes at garage sales. She has donated hundreds of dollars to the organization. The center used her first donation of $142 in 2012 to update their webcams. Now website visitors from all over the world could watch the resident wolves in real time, thanks to Elizabeth.

ONE GIRL HELPING WOLVES

With every sale, Elizabeth hands out promotional bookmarks from the International Wolf Center, her partner in saving wolves. Elizabeth and her family travel there a few times a year to visit. Elizabeth loves spending time with the center's ambassador wolves, Aidan, Denali, Luna, and Boltz, who live there and help educate the public about wolves.

At home, Elizabeth stays in touch with the wolves online (www.wolf.org). Her dream is to become a veterinarian, then live in Ely and care for wolves at the wolf center. It's really important to save wolves, she says. They need our help.

GET INVOLVED!

Helping wolves takes research, creativity, and motivation. Elizabeth took action, and so can you. There are many things you can do to save wolves.

The most important thing to do first is to learn as much as you can. Get information from reputable, unbiased resources. Remember that Internet resources aren't always well researched. Check your facts with multiple sources. Learn as much as you can about wolves so you can form an educated opinion about the issues regarding wolves in the world today and how we can all coexist.

WILD WOLF AIRLINES

Buckle your seatbelts—the flight crews on LightHawk planes fly wild animals all over the United States, Mexico, Central America, and Canada, with help from volunteer pilots and their airplanes.

Like when Cheveya the 11-year-old Mexican gray wolf at the Smithsonian National Zoo needed to catch a nonstop flight to Albuquerque, New Mexico, U.S.A. Without help from LightHawk, the wolf might have had to fly cargo on a commercial flight. Instead, he and the two females in his pack, four-year-old sisters Catella and Nieta, flew aboard a turbo prop plane owned by volunteer pilot Tom Haas. He delivered them on a swift one-way flight from Washington, D.C., to the Wildlife West Nature Park south of Albuquerque.

Zeke the Mexican gray wolf is off-loaded from a LightHawk plane.

When LightHawk transported a rare and highly endangered Mexican gray wolf M1049 (also known as Zeke), a boy named Tyler was also on board. Tyler and his mom (a LightHawk pilot) gave Zeke a lift from the Endangered Wolf Center in St. Louis, Missouri, to Springerville, Arizona, U.S.A., where a service team from the U.S. Fish and Wildlife Service was waiting to transport him to a release location. That day, Tyler wrote a note on the wolf's collar wishing him good luck in the wild.

In May 2013, the organization helped save two genetically valuable newborn Mexican gray wolf pups, rushing them from the Wolf Conservation Center in South Salem, New York, U.S.A., to rescuers at the Mesker Park Zoo in Evansville, Indiana, U.S.A., just hours after they were born. The organization also helps other species, transporting endangered passengers like falcons, loggerhead turtles, and black-footed ferrets.

Make sure you come to your conclusions in an objective manner—that means based on facts rather than feelings. Never assume that someone who has a different opinion is wrong or bad. That doesn't help wolves and shuts down an opportunity for discussion and healthy debate from different sides of an argument. Even if someone has different ideas about how wolves should be managed, listen. Wolves need humans to communicate about all the issues. Take what you know and howl it loud!

EVERYONE CAN HELP

Even ecologically friendly things you do at home are good for wolves and our shared environment. Picking up litter in your neighborhood or at your school, turning off the water while you're brushing your teeth, keeping lights turned off, and eating local food, it all adds up, and they are simple things you can do to reduce the pressure on our natural resources.

You've probably heard the saying "reduce, reuse, recycle." It's an important reminder that every little bit helps. *Reduce* in ways like buying secondhand items instead of new, borrowing books from the library instead of buying new books, and taking only as much food as you'll eat to limit waste. *Reuse* anything you can instead of throwing it away and getting a new one. *Recycle* anything you can by setting out cans and bottles for neighborhood pickup, or exchanging them for cash at a recycling center.

Endangered Species Day (always celebrated on the third Friday of May) is a great reason to help raise awareness in your community about wolves and other endangered species.

If a meat producer is "predator-friendly," like Candll Ranch where Maggie the guard dog lives, it means they use animal husbandry methods—or ways of taking care of their animals—with an emphasis on tolerance. They use nonlethal (not deadly) methods for dealing with depredation practices.

Take action today. Even something small done every day, every week, or every month adds up quickly. Getting involved with helping your world—and the wolves in it—will become a habit you won't want to break. By reading this book, you're already helping to save the beloved wolf.

> THE WORD "TELEMETRY" REFERS TO THE USE OF ELECTRONICS TO LOCATE SOMETHING, LIKE A WOLF BEING LOCATED BY THE SIGNAL EMITTED FROM HIS RADIO COLLAR.

>> ANIMAL RESCUE!

SAVING THE DESERT WOLVES OF INDIA

Defending wolves is not all about science. Wolves connect in unexpected ways with the people who protect them; like the day Dr. Yadvendradev Jhala, a scientist from the Wildlife Institute of India, got in his car to leave for home after a research trip in the flat Bhal area of Gujarat in western India.

His wife, Rajeshwari, was eager to get on the highway for the 900-mile (1,400 km) trip home to Dehradun, India. For more than 20 years, Dr. Jhala has been following his childhood dream of helping to save India's endangered species, like the rare and shy desert wolf, the Asiatic lion, and the tiger.

But something stopped Dr. Jhala before getting on the highway that day. His strong connection to the wild desert wolves of India wouldn't let him go. He can't explain what made him turn

Dr. Yadvendradev Jhala weighs a sedated wolf before he attaches a radio collar and releases the wolf for a study.

the car around and drive six miles (10 km) back into the hot wilderness. Something told him to check a den that contained young pups, just one last time.

But at the den, Dr. Jhala interrupted a group of local farmers. They had stuffed the den with hay and were about to light a match. Dr. Jhala reminded them of the serious consequences of killing the wolf pups.

Months later, Dr. Jhala's students confirmed the survival of the pups who lived to disperse into new territories.

We humans may have more in common with wolves than most people realize.

Conservation tips from Dr. Yadvendradev Jhala, wolf scientist from the Wildlife Institute of India:

1 Learn how to preserve our planet's natural resources—overuse causes species to become extinct.

2 Remember that we share our planet with many other species.

3 Encourage others not to be greedy about using our shared natural resources like water, trees, food, and fuel.

WHEN THE WOLVES AT THE COLUMBUS ZOO IN OHIO WHIFF SUPER-SMELLY FLY REPELLENT ON THEIR BEDDING, THEY SCRATCH, SNIFF, AND ROLL—PROTECTING THEIR EARS *AND* HAVING FUN.

>> CONCLUSION

The black wolf didn't start out as a loner. His parents, Yellowstone wolves #2 and #7 (you read about them on page 98), created the first naturally formed wild pack in the park after their own birth packs had been relocated into Yellowstone in the mid-1990s. He was likely born in one of their last litters.

In October 2009, filmmaker Bob Landis watches the black wolf, #302, set out to patrol his territory, but the old wolf (now ten years old) doesn't return. He lived longer than most, probably because he worked so hard to avoid conflict. Today, wolves in the Blacktail Plateau carry on his legacy. Inspired by his story of perseverance, Landis produced a National Geographic documentary called *The Rise of Black Wolf*.

DNA evidence showed biologists in Yellowstone that the black wolf, with his unusual habits, sired more wolves in Yellowstone than any other wolf, even though he was a pack leader for only one year at the end of his life. Over and over again, he risked his life to breed with females in other packs. Park officials have witnessed many cases where this strategy leads to death.

But #302 was different. Genetic testing and field observations confirm that #302 sired bouncing baby black wolf pups by five different females over the years. The fact that he avoided confrontation may have contributed to his success and long life. For most of it, the black wolf stayed focused on the females and let other males take the lead.

What can we learn from the story of the black wolf? Like us, wolves have families, lessons to learn, work to get done, happy times, and hard times. Wolves have lives—even when we humans aren't looking.

It's time to learn all we can about wolves to help ensure their future. Are you ready to join the pack?

>> RESOURCES

WANT TO LEARN MORE?
Check out these great resources to continue your mission to save wolves!

IN PRINT

Boyer, Crispin. **"Pack Talk."** *National Geographic Kids,* February 2012.

Brandenburg, Jim. ***Brother Wolf: A Forgotten Promise.*** Minocqua, WI: NorthWord Press, 1993.

Brandenburg, Jim. ***White Wolf: Living With an Arctic Legend.*** Minocqua, WI: NorthWord Press, 1990.

Brandenburg, Jim, and Judy Brandenburg. ***Face to Face With Wolves.*** Washington, D.C.: National Geographic Society, 2008.

Chadwick, Douglas. **"Wolf Wars."** *National Geographic,* March 2010.

Dutcher, Jim, and Jamie Dutcher. ***The Hidden Life of Wolves.*** Washington, D.C.: National Geographic Society, 2013.

Grooms, Steve. **"Red Wolf FAQ."** *International Wolf* 17, no. 4 (Winter 2007): 810.

Hutt, Cornelia. **"A Closer Look at Red Wolf Recovery: A Conversation With Dr. David R. Rabon."** *International Wolf* 23, no. 2 (Summer 2013): 812.

Mech, L. David. ***Wolves: Behavior, Ecology, and Conservation.*** Chicago: University of Chicago Press, 2003.

Musgrave, Ruth. **"Wolf Speak."** *National Geographic Kids,* February 2007.

Wang, Xiaoming. ***Dogs: Their Fossil Relatives and Evolutionary History.*** New York: Columbia University Press, 2008.

ONLINE

Defenders of Wildlife

Protects animals and their habitats around the world

www.defenders.org

International Union for Conservation of Nature and Natural Resources (IUCN)

Information on the state of wolves around the world

www.iucnredlist.org

International Wolf Center

Wolf education and news

www.wolf.org

Jim Brandenburg Photo Gallery

Wolf photos and education

www.jimbrandenburg.com

Large Carnivore Initiative for Europe

A specialist group of the IUCN's Species Survival Commission

www.lcie.org

Living With Wolves

Raises awareness about wolves

www.livingwithwolves.org

Minnesota Zoo

Video game that teaches wolf behavior and ecology

www.wolfquest.org

National Geographic Education

Information about history, science, animals, and more

education.nationalgeographic.com/education

National Geographic Kids

Creature features give information on animals from around the world

kids.nationalgeographic.com/kids/animals

National Wildlife Federation

Protects wildlife in the United States

www.nwf.org

United States Fish and Wildlife Service

Follow red wolf recovery efforts

www.fws.gov/redwolf

United States National Park Service

Information about wolves in Yellowstone National Park

www.nps.gov/yell/naturescience/wolves.htm

Wildlife Conservation Trust

Works to protect wildlife around the world

wildlifeconservationtrust.org

World Wildlife Fund

Promotes people living in harmony with wildlife around the world

www.wwf.org

WATCH

"In the Valley of the Wolves." *Nature.* PBS. Produced by Bob Landis and Janet Hess. 2007. (TV documentary)

Living With Wolves/Wolves at Our Door. Produced by Jim Dutcher and Jamie Dutcher. Discovery Channel DVD. 2005. (Documentary)

The Rise of Black Wolf. Nat Geo WILD. 2010. (Documentary)

"Wolf Pack." *National Geographic Explorer.* Directed by Bob Landis. 2003. (TV documentary)

Wolves: A Legend Returns to Yellowstone. National Geographic Video. 2007. (Documentary)

PLACES TO SEE WOLVES AROUND THE WORLD

Alligator River National Wildlife Refuge, Manteo, North Carolina
Blue Range Wolf Recovery Area, Arizona and New Mexico
California Wolf Center, Julian, California
Columbus Zoo and Aquarium, Powell, Ohio
International Wolf Center, Ely, Minnesota
North Carolina Zoo, Asheboro, North Carolina
San Andres National Wildlife Refuge, New Mexico
Smithsonian National Zoological Park, Washington, D.C.
Wolf Conservation Center, South Salem, New York
Wolf Watch UK, Warwickshire, England
Yellowstone National Park, Wyoming

SELECT SCIENTIFIC PAPERS

Read about what scientists are doing today to protect wolves.

Chambers, Steven M., Steven R. Fain, Bud Fazio, and Michael Amaral. "An Account of the Taxonomy of North American Wolves From Morphological and Genetic Analyses." United States Department of the Interior, Fish and Wildlife Service, *North American Fauna* no. 77 (October 2012).

MacNulty, Daniel R., Douglas W. Smith, L. David Mech, and Lynn E. Eberly. "Body Size and Predatory Performance in Wolves: Is Bigger Better?" *Journal of Animal Ecology* 78, no. 3 (May 2009): 532539.

Mech, L. David. "The Challenge and Opportunity of Recovering Wolf Populations." *Conservation Biology* 9, no. 2 (April 1995): 270278.

Mech, L. David. "Is Science in Danger of Sanctifying the Wolf?" *Biological Conservation* 150, no. 1 (June 2012): 143149.

Mech, L. David, and H. Dean Cluff. "Movements of Wolves at the Northern Extreme of the Species' Range, Including During Four Months of Darkness." *PLoS ONE* 6, no. 10 (October 2011): e25328. doi:10.1371/journal .pone.0025328.

ORGANIZATIONS IN THIS BOOK

Blackfoot Challenge
For more information check out page 104.
www.blackfootchallenge.org

California Wolf Center
For more information check out pages 36 and 72.
www.californiawolfcenter.org

International Wolf Center
For more information check out pages 50 and 115.
www.wolf.org

Large Carnivore Education Centre Bulgaria
For more information check out page 93.
www.visitcarnivorebg.org

LightHawk
For more information check out page 115.
www.lighthawk.org

Living With Wolves
For more information check out page 102.
www.livingwithwolves.org

Lobos of the Southwest
For more information check out pages 37–38.
www.mexicanwolves.org

People and Carnivores
For more information check out page 104.
www.peopleandcarnivores.org

Rewilding Europe
For more information check out page 104.
www.rewildingeurope.com

Wolf Conservation Center
For more information check out pages 98 and 115.
www.nywolf.org

Wolves and Moose of Isle Royale
For more information check out pages 37 and 72.
www.isleroyalewolf.org

Wolves of Yellowstone
For more information check out pages throughout.
www.nps.gov/yell/naturescience/wolves.htm

>>INDEX

Boldface indicates illustrations.

A

Activities
    careers **110,** 110–111, **111**
    change the world **94,** 94–95, **95**
    eat like a wolf **76,** 76–77, **77**
    live like a wolf **28,** 28–29, **29**
    map canids **44,** 44–45, **45**
    wolf games **60,** 60–61, **61**
Arctic wolves
    adaptations 35, 70, **70**
    ambassador 98, **98–99**
    Brutus 53, **53**
    camouflage **34–35**
    curiosity **92–93, 108–109**
    range 35
Atka (arctic wolf) 98, **98–99**

B

Bavarian Forest National Park, Germany **82–83**
Black Wolf 10, **10–11,** 12–13
Blacktail Plateau Pack 13
Boitani, Luigi 81, 86, **86**
Brandenburg, Jim 80–81, 105, 108–109, **108–109**
Brutus (arctic wolf) 53, **53**
Bulgaria
    wolf studies 93, **93**
Burras, Elizabeth 115

C

Camouflage **34–35**
Canids
    family tree 32–33, **32–33,** 35
    mapping **44,** 44–45, **45**
Captive wolves **8–9,** 36, **36–37**
Careers **110,** 110–111, **111**
Cassidy, Kira **100–101**
Cave paintings **80–81,** 81
Climate change 89–90

Colors of wolves 18
Communication
    body language **22–23**
    forms of 18
    howling 8, 12, **12–13, 14–15,** 30, **30–31,**
        56–57
    with pack 52, 55
    similarity with dogs 38, **38**
Conservation tips 117
Coyotes 35, 91, **91**

D

Denali National Park, Alaska **24–25, 70–71**
Dens 28, 41, **41**
Depredation 72
Desert wolves 116, **116**
Diet 22, 24
Dire wolves 66, **66–67**
Dogs, domestic 25, **25,** 38, **38,** 91, **91**
Druid Pack 10, 12–13
Dutcher, Jim and Jamie 51–52, **95,** 102, **102, 103**

E

Eastern wolves 33
Eating habits of wolves **74–75,** 106–107, **106–107**
Elk 27, **27**
Endangered Species Act (1973) 43
Ethiopian wolves 35
Europe
    efforts to save wolves 40, 81
    seeing wolves in the wild 102, 104
Expert tips
    conservation tips 117
    creating a powerful message 95
    how you can save wolves 37
    howling 29
    learning about wolves 75, 88
    mapping canids 45
    sharing the story of the wolf 105
    studying wolves 22
    viewing wolves 48
    wildlife careers 111
    wolf games 61
    wolf meals 77

Explorer interviews
  Dan MacNulty 20-21, **20-21**
  Jim Brandenburg 108-109, **108-109**
  L. David Mech 56-57, **56-57**
  Luigi Boitani 86-87, **86-87**

F

Fairy tales 84, **84-85**
Family life **50-51**
Family tree 32-33, **32-33,** 35

G

GPS tracking 12, 19, 27
Gray wolves
  in captivity **8-9**
  eating **48-49, 74-75**
  howling **96-97**
  hunting 46, **46-47, 68-69, 70-71, 73**
  range 18
  reproduction 101
  survival 37

H

Haas, Tom 115
Howling 8, 12, **12-13, 14-15,** 30, **30-31, 56-57**
Humans
  domestication of wolves 83
  encounters with wolves 37-38, 93, **114**
  fear of wolves 80-81, 84
  invasion of wolf territory 37
  livestock 72, 84, 104
  opinions about wolves 43
  worship of wolves 80-81, **80-81, 82-83,**
    83
Hunger 22, 24, 64, 67
Hunting by wolves 62-77
  adaptations 67, 70
  danger to wolves 64
  hunting bison **68-69, 73**
  hunting livestock 72, 84, 90, 91, 104
  hunting moose **70-71**
  hunting woodpecker **71**
  process 71-72
  sense of smell 71

  teamwork 67-68
  teeth characteristics 16, 18
  weaknesses 68
Hunting of wolves 84, 90, **90-91,** 93

I

Ice Age 66, **66-67**
India
  desert wolves 116, **116**
International Wolf Center, Minnesota 50, **50,** 123
Isle Royale National Park, Michigan 72, **72**
Italy
  efforts to save wolves 81

J

Jhala, Yadvendradev 116, **116,** 117

K

Kamots (gray wolf) 51
Keystone species 24-25, 27

L

La Brea Tar Pits, Los Angeles, California 66
Lakota (gray wolf) 51-52
Landis, Bob 10, 58, **58,** 88, 119
Leopold, Aldo 98
Leopold Pack 13, 98, 101
Leptocyon **32**
LightHawk (organization) 115, **115,** 123
Livestock
  hunting by wolves 72, 84, 90, 91, 104
  protection 104, **105,** 106-107
Living With Wolves (organization) 102, 123
Lone wolves 48, 51

M

MI5 (wolf) 87
MacNulty, Dan 20-21, **20-21,** 72, 98, 101
Maggie (livestock guardian dog) 104, 106
Maned wolves 35
Map of wolf ranges 17
Mapping canids **44,** 44-45, **45**
Mech, L. David 48, 50, 53, 57, **57**
Mexican gray wolves **36-37, 39**
  captive breeding 36
  genetics 35, 37

Mexican gray wolves (continued)
    killing livestock 72, 75
    reintroduction into the wild 36, 72, 101
    run-ins with humans 37–38
    survival 38

O

Organizations 123

P

Packs
    communication 52, 55
    as family units **4–5,** 18, 22, 48, 51
    rank 51–52
    search for prey 46, **46–47**
    territory 37–38, 68
Paws 65, **65**
Petitions 94
Petroglyphs **78–79**
Play behavior 16, **16,** 59, **60,** 60–61, **61**
Powers, Jim 107
Prehistoric art **78–79, 80–81,** 81
Pups
    bottle-feeding **95**
    chewing **2–3**
    denning season **58–59**
    early life 55, 59
    eating first **74–75**
    eye color 54
    learning to hunt 59
    mimicking elders **114**
    nursing **42**
    play 16, 59
    red wolves **40–41**

R

Radio collars 34, 53, 93, **93,** 100, **100–101,** 106
Range 43
Range map 17
Red wolves
    breeding program 41
    endangered status 33, 38
    foster program 101–102
    pups **40–41, 42**

    range 18
    reintroduction into the wild 41, 43, 101–102
Reintroduction into the wild
    Mexican gray wolves 36, 72, 101
    red wolves 41, 43, 101–102
Rio (Mexican gray wolf) 36, **36–37,** 72, 75

S

Saving wolves 96–111
    taking action 112–117
    tips 37
Sawtooth Pack 51–52, 102
Scavenging **106**
Senses 26, **26–27,** 55, 71
Size of wolves 16, 18
Smell, sense of 55, 71
Smith, Doug 12, 34, **34,** 37
Stahler, Dan 22, **22**
Submissive behavior 12
Superpowers of wolves
    communication 52, **52**
    place in ecosystem 18, **18**
    similarity to humans 89, **89**

T

Taxonomy 35
Teeth 67
Telemetry
    definition 116
    GPS tracking 12, 19, 27
    radio collars 34, 53, 93, **93,** 100, **100–101,** 106
    satellite collars 87
Territories 37–38, 40
    marking 39, 54, **54–55**
    patrolling **39,** 68
    size 42
Tsingarska, Elena 93, **93**

U

United States
    efforts to save wolves 40–41, 89

V

Vucetich, John 72, **72,** 75

Vucetich, Leah 72

W

Wilson, Seth 104, **104**

Wolves

physical characteristics 16, 18
seeing in the wild 48, 102, 104, **114**
species 18, 33
subspecies 35
vs. domestic dogs 25, **25**

Y

Yellowstone National Park, U.S.
#302 (wolf) **118–119**, 119
#823 (wolf) 19, **19**
black wolf on road **88**
Druids (wolf pack) 10, 12
ecosystem 24–25
Leopold Pack 98, 101
number of wolf packs 13
reintroduction of wolves 98, 101
wolf eating elk **27**
wolves hunting bison **68–69, 73**
Yellowstone Gray Wolf Restoration
Project 34, **34**

Z

Zeke (Mexican gray wolf) **115**

>> IMAGE CREDITS

PHOTO CREDIT ABBREVIATIONS: GI=Getty Images, IS=iStockphoto, MP=Minden Pictures, NGC=National Geographic Creative, SS=Shutterstock

FRONT COVER: Tim Fitzharris **BACK COVER:** Gerry Ellis/Digital Vision **FRONT MATTER:** I, Tom Leeson/NGC; 2-3, Art Wolfe/Iconica/GI; 4-5, Jim and Jamie Dutcher/NGC; 6 (LE), Neal McClimon/IS; 6 (UP), Anup Shah/Taxi/GI; 6 (CTR), Karl Ammann/Digital Vision; 6 (LOLE), Lisa & Mike Husar; 6-7, Matthias Breiter/MP; 6 (RT), Tim Davis/Corbis; 7 (UP), Tim Fitzharris; 7 (CTR), SecondShot/SS; 7 (RT), Darren Moore; 8-9, Daniel J. Cox/NaturalExposures.com; 10, National Geographic Television; 10-11, Pete Benjeyfield; 12-13, Kim Hart **CHAPTER 1:** 14-15, Gerry Ellis/Digital Vision; 16, Jim and Jamie Dutcher/NGC; 18, Terry Biddle; 19, Jimmy Jones; 20-21, courtesy Dan MacNulty; 22, courtesy Dan Stahler; 22-23, Barrett Hedges/NGC; 24-25, John Eastcott & Yva Momatiuk/NGC; 25 (INSET LE), Holly Kuchera/SS; 25 (INSET RT), Utekhina Anna/SS; 26-27, Aspen Photo/SS; 27, Robert Weselmann/NGC; 28 (UP), Cultura RF/GI; 28 (LO), sianc/SS; 29, Design Pics Inc./Alamy **CHAPTER 2:** 30-31, Barrett Hedges/NGC; 32-33, Mauricio Antón/NGC; 34-35, Jim Brandenburg/MP; 34 (INSET), William Campbell/Corbis; 36-37, courtesy California Wolf Center; 38 (UPLE), photogress/IS; 38 (UPRT), eClick/SS; 38 (LOLE), Groomes Photography/IS; 38 (LORT), foaloce/IS; 39, Frans Lanting/NGC; 40-41, Joel Sartore/NGC; 41 (LE), James R. Hearn/SS; 41 (CTR), Critterbiz/SS; 41 (RT), Jim Brandenburg/MP; 42, Joel Sartore/NGC; 43, Gerry Ellis/Digital Vision; 44 (UP), PSL Images/Alamy; 44 (LO), Eric Isselee/SS; 45 (UP), Yellow Dog Productions/The Image Bank/GI; 45 (LO), Epitavi/SS **CHAPTER 3:** 46-47, Jim and Jamie Dutcher/NGC; 48-49, Jim and Jamie Dutcher/NGC; 50 (UP), courtesy International Wolf Center; 50-51, Jim and Jamie Dutcher/NGC; 52, Terry Biddle; 53, courtesy Dr. David Mech; 54-55, Jim and Jamie Dutcher/NGC; 54 (INSET), All Canada Photos/GI; 56-57, Norbert Rosing/NGC; 57 (INSET), courtesy Dr. David Mech; 58 (INSET), National Geographic Television; 58-59, Jim and Jamie Dutcher/NGC; 60 (UP), Marina Jefferson/GI; 60 (LO), iliuta goean/SS; 61 (UP), NuEngine/SS; 61 (LO), PT Images/SuperStock **CHAPTER 4:** 62-63, Joel Sartore/NGC; 64-65, Jim and Jamie Dutcher/NGC; 65, Stuart Armstrong; 66-67, from the collection of the Indiana State Museum and Historic Sites; 68-69, Dan Stahler/NGC; 70-71, John Eastcott & Yva Momatiuk/NGC; 70 (INSET UP), Radius Images/Corbis; 70 (INSET LO), Cybernesco/IS; 71 (RT), Jim and Jamie Dutcher/NGC; 72, courtesy Dr. John Vucetich; 73, Barrett Hodges/NGC; 74-75, Jim and Jamie Dutcher/NGC; 76, Iissart/IS; 76-77, Brand X/GI; 77, Serhan Sidan/IS **CHAPTER 5:** 78-79, Babak Tafreshi/NGC; 80-81, Centre des Monuments Nationaux, France; 82-83, Joel Sartore/NGC; 84-85, Art Resource, NY; 86, courtesy Luigi Boitani; 86-87, Raimund Linke/The Image Bank/GI; 88, Barrett Hedges/NGC; 89, Terry Biddle; 90, Michael Gallacher/NGC; 90-91, Robert Millage/NGC; 91 (1), Cybernesco/IS; 91 (2), Volodymyr Burdiak/SS; 91 (3), skvoor/SS; 91 (4), rashworth/SS; 91 (5), Holly Kuchera/SS; 92-93, Ben Horton/NGC; 93 (INSET), courtesy Elena Tsingarska; 94 (UP), Carol Heesen/SS; 94 (LO), pink_cotton_candy/IS; 95, Jim and Jamie Dutcher/NGC **CHAPTER 6:** 96-97, Norbert Rosing/NGC; 98-99, courtesy Wolf Conservation Center; 100-101, Matt Moyer/NGC; 102, Jim and Jamie Dutcher/NGC; 103, Jim and Jamie Dutcher/NGC; 104, courtesy Seth Wilson; 105, Matthias Hiekel/dpa/Corbis; 106-107, Stuart Armstrong; 108-109, Jim Brandenburg/MP; 109, Jim Brandenburg; 110 (LO), Lisa F. Young/SS; 110 (UP), Dex Image/Alamy; 110 (CTR), AVAVA/SS; 111 (UP notebook), Bennyartist/SS; 111 (UP), KUCO/SS; 111 (CTR), KUCO/SS; 111 (LO), Aleksei Semjonov/SS **CHAPTER 7:** 112-113, Jim and Jamie Dutcher/NGC; 114, kochanowski/SS; 115, U.S. Fish and Wildlife Service; 116, courtesy Yadvendradev Jhala, Ph.D.; 117, Jim and Jamie Dutcher/NGC; 118-119, Kim Hart; 120-121, Marina Jay/SS; 122, belizar/SS

From page 7: $10.00 donation to National Geographic Society. Charges will appear on your wireless bill or be deducted from your prepaid balance. All purchases must be authorized by account holder. Must be 18 years of age or have parental permission to participate. Message and data rates may apply. Text STOP to 50555 to STOP. Text HELP to 50555 for HELP. Full terms: www.mGive.org/T

For everyone who loves wolves, especially those in my own pack: Guy, Max, and Quinn. —K. J.

For Elizabeth (GG) Cook, Menah, Seb, Mushroom, Ziggy, and Georgie. —D. R. E.

Thanks to Kate Olesin and Jennifer Emmett for giving me the opportunity to write this book and to *National Geographic Kids* magazine senior editor Catherine Hughes for recommending me for the project. Thanks also to Daniel Raven-Ellison and everyone in the children's book division who, by collaborating to create this book, are all helping to save wolves.

And thanks to Dan MacNulty, Doug Smith, Dan Stahler, David Mech, John Vucetich, Luigi Boitani, Jim Brandenburg, Bob Landis, Steve Primm, and all the other scientists, conservationists, and wolf lovers who study and protect wolves. The stories and insight that you've shared with me have been like wolf tracks in the snow, guiding me on the path to writing this book. I am privileged to share what I've learned about wolves with young readers. —K. J.

Published by the National Geographic Society
John M. Fahey, *Chairman of the Board and Chief Executive Officer*
Declan Moore, *Executive Vice President; President, Publishing and Travel*
Melina Gerosa Bellows, *Publisher and Chief Creative Officer, Books, Kids, and Family*

Prepared by the Book Division
Hector Sierra, *Senior Vice President and General Manager*
Nancy Laties Feresten, *Senior Vice President, Kids Publishing and Media*
Jennifer Emmett, *Vice President, Editorial Director, Children's Books*
Eva Absher-Schantz, *Design Director, Kids Publishing and Media*
Jay Sumner, *Director of Photography, Children's Publishing*
R. Gary Colbert, *Production Director*
Jennifer A. Thornton, *Director of Managing Editorial*

Staff for This Book
Kate Olesin, *Project Editor*
Eva Absher-Schantz, *Art Director*
Lori Epstein, *Senior Photo Editor*
Em Dash Design, *Designer*
Ariane Szu-Tu, *Editorial Assistant*
Callie Broaddus, *Design Production Assistant*
Margaret Leist, *Photo Assistant*
Carl Mehler, *Director of Maps*
Sven M. Dolling, *Map Research and Production*
Grace Hill, *Associate Managing Editor*
Michael O'Connor, *Production Editor*
Lewis R. Bassford, *Production Manager*
Susan Borke, *Legal and Business Affairs*

Production Services
Phillip L. Schlosser, *Senior Vice President*
Chris Brown, *Vice President, NG Book Manufacturing*
George Bounelis, *Senior Production Manager*
Nicole Elliott, *Director of Production*
Rachel Faulise, *Manager*
Robert L. Barr, *Manager*

The National Geographic Society is one of the world's largest nonprofit scientific and educational organizations. Founded in 1888 to "increase and diffuse geographic knowledge," the Society's mission is to inspire people to care about the planet. It reaches more than 400 million people worldwide each month through its official journal, *National Geographic*, and other magazines; National Geographic Channel; television documentaries; music; radio; films; books; DVDs; maps; exhibitions; live events; school publishing programs; interactive media; and merchandise. National Geographic has funded more than 10,000 scientific research, conservation and exploration projects and supports an education program promoting geographic literacy.

For more information, please visit nationalgeographic.com, call 1-800-NGS LINE (647-5463), or write to the following address:
National Geographic Society
1145 17th Street N.W.
Washington, D.C. 20036-4688 U.S.A.

Visit us online at nationalgeographic.com/books

For librarians and teachers: ngchildrensbooks.org

More for kids from National Geographic: kids.nationalgeographic.com

For information about special discounts for bulk purchases, please contact National Geographic Books Special Sales: ngspecsales@ngs.org

For rights or permissions inquiries, please contact National Geographic Books Subsidiary Rights: ngbookrights@ngs.org

Trade paperback ISBN: 978-1-4263-1494-0
Reinforced library edition: 978-1-4263-1495-7

Printed in China

14/PPS/1